Levine's information reveals, among other things, that students today are overwhelmingly materialistic, cynical about society and its institutions (including higher education), and so competitive about grades that they condone cheating. More significantly, their aspirations are inward, personal, and individualistic rather than social and humanitarian, reflecting the "me first" philosophy that currently pervades the nation. These findings will be crucial for all who want to help students attain their educational goals—and for those who want to develop strategies for redirecting students' often overly self-centered pursuits.

THE AUTHOR

ARTHUR LEVINE is senior fellow at The Carnegie Foundation for the Advancement of Teaching in Washington, D.C.

WHEN DREAMS AND HEROES DIED

*A Portrait
of Today's
College Student*

PREPARED FOR THE CARNEGIE COUNCIL
ON POLICY STUDIES IN HIGHER EDUCATION

Arthur Levine

WHEN DREAMS
AND HEROES DIED

A Portrait
of Today's
College Student

Jossey-Bass Publishers
San Francisco • Washington • London • 1980

WHEN DREAMS AND HEROES DIED
A Portrait of Today's College Student
Arthur Levine

Copyright © 1980 by: The Carnegie Foundation
for the Advancement of Teaching

Jossey-Bass Inc., Publishers
433 California Street
San Francisco, California 94104

Jossey-Bass Limited
28 Banner Street
London EC1Y 8QE

Copies are available from Jossey-Bass, San Francisco,
for the United States and Possessions, and for Canada,
Australia, New Zealand, and Japan.
Copies for the rest of the world are available
from Jossey-Bass, London.

Library of Congress Cataloging in Publication Data

Levine, Arthur.
    When dreams and heroes died.

    Bibliography: p. 148
    Includes index.
    1. College students — United States — Attitudes.
2. Narcissism.   I. Carnegie Council on Policy
Studies in Higher Education.   II. Title.
LA229.L42   378'.1981'0973   80-8005
ISBN 0-87589-481-X

Manufactured in the United States of America

JACKET DESIGN BY WILLI BAUM

FIRST EDITION

Code 8042

The Carnegie Council Series

The following publications are available from Jossey-Bass Inc., Publishers, 433 California Street, San Francisco, California 94104.

The Federal Role in Postsecondary Education: Unfinished Business, 1975-1980
The Carnegie Council on Policy Studies in Higher Education

More Than Survival: Prospects for Higher Education in a Period of Uncertainty
The Carnegie Foundation for the Advancement of Teaching

Low or No Tuition: The Feasibility of a National Policy for the First Two Years of College
The Carnegie Council on Policy Studies in Higher Education

Making Affirmative Action Work in Higher Education: An Analysis of Institutional and Federal Policies with Recommendations
The Carnegie Council on Policy Studies in Higher Education

The States and Higher Education: A Proud Past and a Vital Future
The Carnegie Foundation for the Advancement of Teaching

Faculty Bargaining in Public Higher Education: A Report and Two Essays
The Carnegie Council on Policy Studies in Higher Education, Joseph W. Garbarino, David E. Feller, Matthew W. Finkin

Presidents Confront Reality: From Edifice Complex to University Without Walls
Lyman A. Glenny, John R. Shea, Janet H. Ruyle, Kathryn H. Freschi

Progress and Problems in Medical and Dental Education: Federal Support Versus Federal Control
The Carnegie Council on Policy Studies in Higher Education

Managing Multicampus Systems: Effective Administration in an Unsteady State
Eugene C. Lee, Frank M. Bowen

Challenges Past, Challenges Present: An Analysis of American Higher Education Since 1930
David D. Henry

Educational Leaves for Employees: European Experience for American Consideration
Konrad von Moltke, Norbert Schneevoigt

Next Steps for the 1980s in Student Financial Aid: A Fourth Alternative
The Carnegie Council on Policy Studies in Higher Education

The following technical reports were published by the Carnegie Council on Policy Studies in Higher Education.

The States and Higher Education:
A Proud Past and a Vital Future
SUPPLEMENT to a Commentary of
The Carnegie Foundation for the
Advancement of Teaching
*The Carnegie Foundation for the
Advancement of Teaching*

A Classification of Institutions
of Higher Education: Revised
Edition
*The Carnegie Council on Policy
Studies in Higher Education*

Changing Practices in
Undergraduate Education
*Robert Blackburn, Ellen
Armstrong, Clifton Conrad,
James Didham, Thomas McKune*

Carnegie Council National
Surveys 1975–76: Aspects of
American Higher Education
(Vol. 1)
Martin Trow

Aspects of American
Higher Education, 1969–1975
Martin Trow

Carnegie Council National
Surveys 1975–76: Faculty
Marginals (Vol. 2)
*The Carnegie Council on Policy
Studies in Higher Education*

Carnegie Council National
Surveys 1975–76: Undergraduate
Marginals (Vol. 3)
*The Carnegie Council on Policy
Studies in Higher Education*

Carnegie Council National
Surveys 1975–76: Graduate
Student Marginals (Vol. 4)
*The Carnegie Council on Policy
Studies in Higher Education*

Enrollment and Cost Effect of
Financial Aid Plans for Higher
Education
Joseph Hurd

Market Conditions and Tenure for
Ph.D's in U.S. Higher Education:
Results from the 1975 Carnegie
Faculty Survey and Comparison
with Results from the 1973 ACE
Survey
Charlotte V. Kuh

Field Disaggregated Analysis
and Projections of Graduate
Enrollment and Higher Degree
Production
Christoph von Rothkirch

A Degree for College Teachers:
The Doctor of Arts
*Paul L. Dressel, Mary Magdala
Thompson*

Market Conditions and Tenure in
U.S. Higher Education 1955–1973
Charlotte V. Kuh, Roy Radner

U.S. Faculty After the Boom:
Demographic Projections to 2000
Luis Fernandez

Preserving the Lost Generation:
Policies to Assure a Steady Flow
of Young Scholars Until the Year
2000
Roy Radner, Charlotte V. Kuh

Observations on the Relations
Between Education and Work
in the People's Republic of
China: Report of a Study
Group, 1978
Clark Kerr, Chairman

Contents

Foreword

In this book, Arthur Levine draws upon carefully collected data from many sources to give us a portrait of the college generation of the 1970s. In contrast to the generation of the 1960s, this one has been considered quiescent. It is also described in contradictory terms—optimistic and pessimistic, idealistic and pragmatic, liberal and conservative. Such contradictions can be bewildering until we discover, as Dr. Levine points out, that they often refer to different things. Students are optimistic, for example, about their own futures yet pessimistic about the future of their country. They are idealistic about the kind of world they would like to live in but pragmatic about making it in the world they have to live in. They are liberal about social trends and life-styles but more conservative than they once were about political issues. Such distinctions are helpful in understanding this generation, but many readers will find them also disturbing.

Dr. Levine seeks to explain the discontinuity between the preoccupations of students in the 1960s and those he describes as characteristic of students of the 1970s. His title and his discussion suggest that the discontinuity occurred because, for the student generation of the 1970s, the bright illusions about American society were lost. They were tarnished by the misdeeds and duplicity of the nation's leadership, weakened by the impotency of the very political system the earlier college generation attempted to reshape for its own ends, and darkened by the loss of heroes who believed and taught that the illusions—the ideals—of the generation need not be abandoned.

The antidote Dr. Levine prescribes for a generation of people afflicted with too little hope for humanity and too much concern for themselves is more attention to liberal education as a component of the college experience. If adopted, his recommendation for reincorporating the liberal arts in the college curriculum will not help the generation he is writing about in this study. That generation is now beyond the reach of the proposal. But it might possibly make a difference for future generations by helping them to shape new dreams.

This book has been prepared as a technical report for the Carnegie Council on Policy Studies in Higher Education. It is rich in data about students collected from many sources, including special surveys and studies conducted or sponsored by the Council staff itself. The Council is deeply appreciative of Arthur Levine's efforts to bring this data together in a provocative and useful way and for sharing with us his personal conclusions about their meaning and the consequences they suggest for the future.

CLARK KERR
Chairman
The Carnegie Council on Policy
Studies in Higher Education

DOONESBURY
by Garry Trudeau

Preface

A friend of mine, Jane Lichtman, sent me the Doonesbury cartoon on the opposite page more than three years ago after receiving the earliest outline for this book. I knew then that I would use it as the frontispiece for the volume. It would make for a humorous introduction. But as my research progressed, the strip became an increasingly serious matter: not only because it is depressing to try to write a book while worrying whether anyone will take time to read it but also because my research yielded conclusions so much more disheartening and sad than those I had anticipated.

In this book, I aim to paint as accurate and candid a portrait of today's college students as possible. It is a volume about the students who went to college in the 1970s, though the emphasis is on the latter part of the decade. The research was a labor of love, begun in part to cut through the many myths about the students who are attending college today and in part to see how students have actually changed since the 1960s.

I suspected that some things were different. I worked across the street from the University of California campus in Berkeley. Strolling out of the university's main library one day, I was handed a leaflet announcing a demonstration against the university's South African investment policy. I decided to do a bit of field research and take a look. As I approached Sproul Plaza, the site of the demonstration announced in the leaflet and the center of much of Berkeley's unrest during the 1960s, I noticed that the plaza was full of people—more than I had ever seen there before. On closer examination, however, there proved to be two groups. In one, a crowd of several hundred, many were applauding wildly, while a few were even jumping up and down. The other group, much more somber, consisted of perhaps fifty people, some sitting on the steps of the administration building, others marching in a very small circle. It turned out that the large group was listening to a blue grass band, while the smaller assembly was the demonstration. I asked the music aficionados if they were part of the protest. They assured me that they were not. I asked why. The answers from my small unscientific sample broke down neatly into four categories—one for each respondent—"I don't care," "I don't have the time," "I have too much homework," and "I really like the music."

This did not seem to be the radical Berkeley that I had heard and read about in the 1960s. I chalked it up to a "return to normalcy" among undergraduates. Throughout the seventies, commentators described the nation's campuses as in the throes of a 1950s revival. That seemed about right, and this is what I expected would be borne out by my research.

But, as I said at the outset, I was surprised. The following pages describe the generation of students attending college today.

Chapter One examines popular conceptions of the college student of the 1960s and the 1970s. The tendency toward stereotyping is discussed, and an overview of the differences between today's students and their counterparts of a decade ago is provided.

The second chapter looks at changes during recent years in the nation, the family, the schools, and the media. In combination, these changes have caused a shift in the mood of college students and in the nation as a whole, a shift that has been referred to elsewhere as the new meism or new narcissism.

Chapter Three deals with politics. Student activism is by no means dead, but the theme of this chapter is cynicism, distrust, apathy, the rise of self-interest political groups, and the growth of student influence on and off campus. In large measure, all of this is the legacy of the Vietnam/Watergate era.

Education is discussed in Chapter Four. Students today are weaker in the three Rs—reading, writing, and arithmetic. They are more career-oriented and more competitive, and they receive higher grades than did their predecessors of the 1960s.

The fifth chapter is concerned with student social life. Campus-based activity is definitely down. What is "in" and what is "out" has, of course, changed appreciably over the decade. Diversity, individualism, escapism, and a search for something to believe in are the dominant characteristics of student social life today.

Chapter Six talks of the future. Undergraduates today are acquisitive and determined to fulfill the American dream. They are optimistic about their personal futures but very pessimistic about the future of the country. The fear of being victimized is widespread.

The final chapter discusses student characteristics that have remained the same through nearly 350 years of college history, characteristics that have oscillated or changed from time to time, and characteristics that are unique to this generation. Future prospects are also considered. The chapter concludes with a recommendation.

Some of what I learned in this study was saddening. Particularly disconcerting was the long-lasting and profoundly negative impact exerted by the Vietnam War, the turbulence of the 1960s, and the Watergate era on today's college students. The level of altruism among current undergraduates is low. It has been replaced by an ethic of "looking out for number one" and an almost singleminded concern with material success. In part, this is a reflection of the mood of the times, but it is also encouraged, often unwittingly, by actions of the family, the schools, the media, and the government. This point is developed throughout the volume.

I was disturbed by the overwhelming sense of meism that I encountered among students. It permeates all aspects of the undergraduate world, from politics to education to social life to the future that students envision. Today's meism grows out of a generalized cynicism, lack of trust, and fear among students, and it promises a continuation of such attitudes.

Meism as I found it in this study is an illness, a socially divisive and individually isolating disease. It arises when the social contract between a society and its people begins to break down or when the social contract is perceived by the populace as breaking down. In its mildest form, meism is a periodic event, common to all communities. Ironically, it is an attitude shared by the lonely. Meism separates people. In the extreme, it robs them of their ability to see common problems and to work together for common solutions. The problems grow worse, and people feel victimized, coming to view their problems as a form of personal harrassment. The feeling of impotence rises, and apathy increases. All in all, it is a classic prescription for poisoning a democratic society.

Meism is what made the Doonesbury cartoon a serious matter for me. Though there has been considerable national discussion on the subject, including a presidential address on malaise, it appears that the roots of the problem and the nature of the phenomenon have not been fully understood. We fail to realize the extent or even the ways in which meism permeates the current college generation and our society as a whole. So far as the nation's campuses are concerned, wracked as they were by years of student unrest, there has been a tendency to equate the recent quiet with well-being. Like many other people, I seriously misjudged the post-1960s college generation.

This volume is based upon studies conducted under the auspices of the Carnegie Commission and Carnegie Council on Policy Studies in Higher Education, including national surveys of undergraduates in 1969 and 1976 and a 1978 survey of nearly 600 schools representing a cross section of American higher education on institutional and student changes since 1969. In addition, during visits in 1979 to twenty-six colleges and universities reflecting the diversity of this nation's institutions of higher education, a round table discussion was conducted with a group of intentionally varied undergraduates. A ranking student government official or the student newspaper editor was interviewed as well. In addition, extensive use was made of the Cooperative Institutional Research Program's annual studies of college freshmen. Additional details about each of these studies will be found in Appendix A.

Despite the volume of data, I have tried to keep this study short and to write in a popular rather than an academic style in the hope of discrediting Doonesbury and getting some "people to sit through it."

I had a great deal of help in writing this book. Clark Kerr and the Carnegie Council offered constructive comments on outlines and subsequent drafts. Members of the Carnegie Council staff, including C. E. Christian, Sandra Elman, John Shea, and Verne Stadtman, assisted by making campus site visits. Despite extended time on the road and tight deadlines, they did an outstanding job. Nan Sand, the Council librarian, expedited my work in ways too numerous to list. Sandra Loris was an excellent secretary, always meeting another deadline. Somehow she took a mass of scribbled paper and miraculously turned it into a book. Maresi Nerad, Rachel Volberg, and Keith Wilson worked as research assistants on this study; not only did they make an important contribution to the book, but the study was more enjoyable for their friendship. Linda Fentiman, my best friend and my wife, listened to me rant and rave throughout the research and writing of this book. She puffed me up when I was down and deflated me when I was cocky. In the process I gained five pounds. I thank them all. I am also grateful to the roughly two thousand faculty members and administrators who participated in this study, as well as the tens of thousands of student participants, particularly those who spent hours in group interviews.

This book is dedicated to my parents, Katherine and Meyer Levine, with love and gratitude.

Washington, D.C.   Arthur Levine
June 1980

The Author

Arthur Levine is senior fellow at The Carnegie Foundation for the Advancement of Teaching in Washington, D.C. He received a B.A. degree in biology from Brandeis University (1970) and a Ph.D. degree in sociology and in higher education from the State University of New York at Buffalo (1976).

Before joining The Carnegie Foundation, Levine spent five years with the Carnegie Council on Policy Studies in Higher Education in Berkeley, California. His prior work experience includes a variety of positions such as Congressional staffer, public school teacher, and university lecturer.

Levine's previous books include *Reform of Undergraduate Education* (1973, coauthored with John Weingart), which received the American Council on Education Book of the Year Award in 1974, *Handbook on Undergraduate Education* (1978), and *Why Innovation Fails* (1980). He directed the Carnegie Council study on ethics in higher education that resulted in the volume, *Fair Practices in Higher Education: Rights and Responsibilities of Students and Their Colleges in a Period of Intensified Competition for Enrollments* (1979). Levine is a frequent consultant and speaker on the subject of undergraduate curriculum and ethical practice in higher education.

WHEN DREAMS AND HEROES DIED

A Portrait
of Today's
College Student

PREPARED FOR THE CARNEGIE COUNCIL
ON POLICY STUDIES IN HIGHER EDUCATION

1

In the Shadow of the 1960s

"We're not real college kids like the people who went to school in the 1960s."

Today's college student is different from the student I went to college with in the late 1960s. When I think about how, what comes to mind is a 1974 student newspaper series on campus changes since the sixties (*The Spectrum,* State University of New York at Buffalo). Most memorable were four drawings depicting the college students of the 1960s and the 1970s. The male of the sixties had long hair and a scraggly beard; he carried a Molotov cocktail in one hand and held the other clenched above his head. His counterpart of several years later struck the same pose, but his hair was styled, the Molotov cocktail was replaced by a diploma, and the clenched fist clutched a wad of dollar bills. The female of the sixties had loose, disheveled hair and wore a work shirt; she carried a brick and stood beside a broken window. A few years later, smartly dressed and coiffed, she had traded the brick for a book and was standing beside an employment office window.

This sort of imagery has been reproduced in motion pictures. In my generation, the college student hero—or anti-hero, as the case may be—was Benjamin Braddock, of *The Graduate,* as played by Dustin Hoffman. In that film, Benjamin, the son of a wealthy Southern California lawyer, was an honor student, an athlete, and editor of the yearbook at an Ivy League school. After graduation, he returned home to face a world depicted as tawdry in its wealth, hypocritical in its personal relationships, and lacking in meaningful life choices. These themes were underlined in a musical score by Paul Simon and Art Garfunkle. Their song "The Sounds of Silence" was concerned with crass commercialism and the inability of people to communicate with one another. It tells of "people talking without speaking," "people hearing without listening," and people "praying to a neon god they made." Another song, "Big Green Pleasure Machine," counseled that for every problem—whether it be authority figures, sleeplessness, getting fired, hippies, cavities, bounced checks, or a pregnant girl friend—there was a commercial remedy—packaged solutions, canned fun. And a third song, "Mrs. Robinson," highlighted the lack of choices, the demise of common values, and the loss of national heroes.

> Going to the candidates' debate
> Laugh about it
> Talk about it
> When you've got to choose
> Every way you look at it you lose
> Where have you gone Joe DiMaggio
> A nation turns its lonely eyes to you

The movie setting alternates between Southern California and Berkeley. Berkeley is portrayed unsympathetically as a city composed of preppy fraternity types, jocks, and an ignorant populace that fears outside agitators while ignoring the problems raised by their own protesting children. Every social institution Benjamin encounters is ridiculed, including several of the fundamentals—the family, marriage, and the church. In the final sequence, Benjamin runs away from it all on a city bus with a woman who, just moments before, had married another man. To accomplish this feat, the hero must impersonate a minister, disrupt a wedding ceremony, fight off the young woman's cursing family and friends, and lock them all in a church, using a large cross to bar the door.

By 1978, Benjamin Braddock had left the scene, taking

with him his alienation and uncertainties, and Joe DiMaggio had returned to sell coffeemakers. Back also was Joe College and fraternity life, complements of *Animal House,* a product of the *National Lampoon.* With them came a new characterization of the college student, more traditional and more popular than Benjamin Braddock. So successful was *Animal House* that three new television shows—"Coed Fever", "Brothers and Sisters", and "Delta House"—were cloned in its wake, one prime time series for each of the three major networks. The residents of *Animal House* could not be more different from Benjamin Braddock. While Benjamin is naive, academic, intellectual, and serious with a capital S, they are an anti-intellectual, worldly-wise, rowdy, and hard-partying group whose toga parties and food fights were emulated on real campuses all over the country. By the end of *Animal House* all of its members have flunked out of Faber College, which had as its motto "Knowledge is Good." Where Benjamin engaged in a courtship that was unphysical and entirely intellectual—spent, following his true love from class to class, asking why she would not marry him—romance at *Animal House* is spiritual (about 96 proof) and carnal, and classes never get in the way of love. While Benjamin ultimately tries to run away from society, the heroes of *Animal House* do not even consider it evil. In fact, they reap the best of its rewards. The most dissipated of the lot, John "Buffalo" Blutarsky—who communicates primarily by grunting and who uses his head largely as a beer can compactor—becomes a U.S. senator. Others become doctors, lawyers, and *est* trainers. Like the film, the music is nostalgic, and its themes are traditional and pragmatic. "Hey Paula" tells of yearning to marry when school is through: "True love means planning our life for two." "Wonderful World" extolls the virtues of romance over book learning. The singer does a quick gloss over of his academic repertoire, noting in passing that he does not know much about history, trigonometry, algebra, geography, biology, or French, but he does know about love. In fact, although he is not an "A" student, which is not surprising in view of his academic deficiencies, he would become one if that was necessary to win the woman he loves. And "Money (That's What I Want)" puts everything in perspective.

> The best things in life are free
> But you can give that to the birds and the bees
> Your love it gives me such a thrill
> But your love it don't pay the bills
> Money don't get everything it's true
> But what it don't get I can't use.

Myth and Reality of Student Generations

There is only one weakness, albeit a serious one, in these characterizations of the college student: They do not correspond to the students I knew in the late 1960s or the students I met on campuses throughout the country in the 1970s. These images are caricatures. And every college generation has been so portrayed—students of the 1920s as wet, wild, and wicked; students of the 1930s as somber and radical; students of the 1940s as mature and "in a hurry"; students of the 1950s as silent; and students of the 1960s as angry and activist. Generational images reflect the characteristics that make the college students of one era different from their predecessors whether they be jazz, flapper fashions, the Charleston, women smoking, and hip flasks of the twenties or jeans, beards, acid rock music, demonstrations, and marijuana of the sixties. These generational images emphasize newly emerging trends—not universal practices or even majority behavior.

With time and distance, generational images evolve into caricatures and myths. The reality of the sixties has already begun to fade, as much for those of us who attended college then as for those who watched the decade pass by on television and those who went to college in their aftermath. As years have passed, the students of the sixties have grown larger than life, their concerns have become more altruistic, and their commitment to change has been exaggerated. The fact of the matter is that in 1969 only 28 percent of college students had participated in a demonstration of any type while in college (Gallup International, 1969), and during the week of the most widespread campus unrest in history following the Kent and Jackson State shootings, 43 percent of the nation's colleges and universities were unaffected (Peterson and Bilorusky, 1971, p. 15). Like other periods, the sixties had their share of athletes, fraternity members, and vocationally oriented students, so it should not be surprising that half (49 percent) of all undergraduates in 1969 saw the chief benefit of a college education as increased earning power (Carnegie Surveys, 1969).

There is a temptation to compare the present with our recollections of the past. Real events are dwarfed by the shadows of yesteryear. And real people seem bloodless by comparison, both to themselves and to others.

I was shocked and surprised at the extent to which today's college students compare themselves to the mythical creature who walked our campuses a decade ago. I was told with sadness more times than I care to remember, "We're not real college kids like the people who went to school in the 1960s." Even more frequently, I was asked what it had been like to go to college in the "golden days." For a number of students, there was a deep sense that they had missed something. And they did miss something, years that for me were very special, but unfortunately for them what they imagined they had missed was very often overblown or fantasized.

Myths can be damaging. Bearing in mind this and Simone Signoret's observation, *Nostalgia Isn't What It Used to Be* (1978), the myth of the 1960s college student should be left behind. As an epitaph it might simply be acknowledged that if today's college students seem puny in the shadow of the recollected 1960s, so too would the actual students of that decade in comparison to the myths that have grown up about them.

Nonetheless, real differences do exist between college students today and their counterparts of the 1960s. Three changes stand out.

First, the number of college students has increased substantially. In fall 1969, 7,976,834 students were attending

American colleges and universities. By 1979, the number had risen to 11,669,429, an increase of 42 percent (National Center for Educational Statistics, 1969, 1979). With growth there have been significant changes in student attendance patterns. The population attending college part-time shot up from 31 percent in 1969 to 41 percent in 1979 (National Center for Education Statistics, 1969, 1979). In fact, more than half of all undergraduates (54 percent) worked at jobs while attending college and two out of five (41 percent) attended at least some of their classes at night. Today's students are also more likely to drop out of college or stop out for a term, or longer: In 1969, 17 percent of undergraduates stopped out, versus 26 percent in 1976. In addition, today's students attend more than one college in greater frequency than their predecessors, the proportion doing so rose from 24 percent in 1969 to 34 percent in 1976 (Carnegie Surveys, 1969, 1976).

Second, the composition of the student body has changed. High-achieving young people from wealthier families, with better-educated parents are, as in the 1960s, most likely to attend college. However, increases have been registered in the proportion of enrollment from traditionally underrepresented minority groups—blacks (from 7 percent in 1969 to 11 percent in 1976), women (from 28 percent in 1969 to 51 percent in 1979), and adults 25 and over (from 28 percent in 1972 to 35 percent in 1977), among others (National Center for Education Statistics, 1969, 1979). The spread of these students throughout the various institutions of higher education has been uneven, with different types of colleges and universities accommodating disparate clienteles. The champagne institutions, consisting of the most research-oriented universities, such as Berkeley, Michigan, Yale, and Harvard, and the most selective liberal arts colleges, such as Reed, Amherst, and Vassar, remain the home of the traditional student, while two-year colleges have absorbed much of the influx of "new" students, as shown in Table 1.

Table 1. Characteristics of undergraduates in degree programs at community and junior colleges, the most selective liberal arts colleges, and the most research-oriented universities

	Community and junior colleges	Most selective liberal arts colleges	Most research-oriented universities
Modal parents' income	$10,000–$14,999	$35,000 or more	$35,000 or more
Median father's education	High school graduate	College graduate	College graduate
Modal high school grade point average	B	B+	A, A+
Percent of undergraduates who are nonwhite	20	8	9
Percent of undergraduates who are 25 years of age or older	45	4	11
Percent of undergraduates working full-time	35	3	6
Percent of undergraduates who are married	43	5	11
Percent of undergraduates who are veterans	21	1	5

Source: Carnegie Surveys, 1976.

Third, student character has changed. When student personnel administrators at 586 colleges and universities were given a list of 52 words and phrases and asked to describe how students on their campus had changed since 1969–70, they said that students were more career-oriented (on 71 percent of the campuses), better groomed (on 57 percent of the campuses), more concerned with material success (on 54 percent of the campuses), more concerned with self (on 44 percent of the campuses), and more practical (on 40 percent of the campuses). Students were also less radical (on 58 percent of the campuses), less activist (on 57 percent of the campuses), and less hostile (on 40 percent of the campuses). To describe the majority of undergraduates at their institution, most administrators selected just five phrases: career-oriented (84 percent), concerned with self (73 percent), concerned with material success (63 percent), well groomed (57 percent), and practical (55 percent) (Carnegie Surveys, 1978).

The next chapter will discuss the formative precollege experience of today's students.

2

The Making of the Current College Generation

"Everything is bad. People only care about me, me, me!"

In 1961, John Kennedy captured the popular imagination when he summoned his fellow Americans to "ask not what your country can do for you, but what you can do for your country." Seventeen years later, Californian Howard Jarvis won the plaudits of the nation when he led a successful tax revolt premised on the notion that citizens were being asked to do too much for their country. Each was recognized as a "man on horseback" for his time.

The "man on horseback" is part leader and part follower. He or she is as much, if not more, a product of the public mood as the creator of that mood. Howard Jarvis began preaching his message of individual rights contemporaneously with John Kennedy's exhortation of individual responsibility to the community. For the Jarvis philosophy to eclipse the Kennedy position has required a fundamental shift in the American world view—a basic change in our conception of the national community and our place in it.

The years of the Kennedy administration are mythologized today as "a brief and shining moment in Camelot." The spirit of Camelot persisted into the early Johnson years when the characteristics that accompanied it

—the sense of voluntarism, the perception of mutuality of individual and community interest, and the belief in the individual's ability to profit from cooperation with the community—began a precipitous slide, which has continued to the present. Since the slide began America has been in a state of increasing pessimism and declining community.

This is borne out in the polls. Between 1959 and 1964, national expectations about our personal futures and the future of our country rose, but after 1964 both began to drop, and both reached lows in 1979. What is especially important to note though is that personal expectations have fallen just slightly, while expectations for the nation have plummeted. This is shown in Figure 1.

A majority of adult Americans now believe that what they think does not count for much; that the people running the country do not really care what happens to them; that public leaders do not know what they are doing; that the rich get richer and the poor get poorer; and that government wastes a lot of money. Since 1964, the percentage of people reporting such opinions saw a dramatic increase, as shown in Table 2.

Confidence in the leaders of major social institutions, including medicine, higher education, organized religion, the U.S. Supreme Court, the military, major companies, the executive branch of government, the press, Congress, organized labor, and advertising agencies, declined from an average of 45 percent in 1966 to an average of 21 percent in 1979. This is shown in Table 3.

The prognosis for the future is gloomy. In January 1980, 83 percent of the adults surveyed believed that it was likely that the United States would be at war within the next three years—a 48 percentage point increase in seventeen months (*Public Opinion,* April-May 1980, p. 21). In other surveys, 65 percent of Americans thought the United States was falling behind the Soviet Union, and 58 percent said that this country was less respected around the world than it had been ten years before (*Public Opinion,* March-May 1979, p. 22). More than 90 percent believed that if there were

Figure 1. Five years from now: State of the nation and personal life, 1959–1979

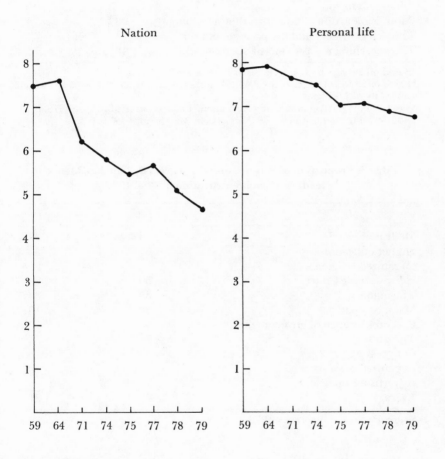

Nation   Personal life

Note: Respondents were asked to note the state of the nation and of their own lives five years hence using a scale of 0 (worst) to 10 (best). Data from 1959 through 1974 were obtained by The Gallup Organization from 1,500 interviews per survey. Later data from Caddell's Cambridge Survey is based on 1,500 to 2,000 interviews.
Source: Adapted from *Newsweek,* August 6, 1979, p. 27. © *Newsweek* Magazine. Used by permission.

Table 2. Changing American attitudes from the mid-1960s to 1977

	1964	1966	1977
What you think doesn't count much any more[a]		37%	61%
People running the country don't really care what happens to you[a]		26	60
Public leaders don't know what they are doing[b]	28%		52
The rich get richer and the poor get poorer[a]		45	77
The government wastes lots of tax money[b]	48		76

[a]Based on surveys by Louis Harris and Associates.
[b]Based on surveys by Center for Political Studies of the Institute for Social Research, University of Michigan.
Source: "Louis Harris Finds Rising Alienation," *Public Opinion,* May-June 1978, p. 23; and "Growing Skepticism. . . ," *Public Opinion,* March-April 1978, p. 23.

Table 3. Proportion of Americans with a great deal of confidence in leaders of social institutions: 1966, 1979

	1966	1979
Medicine	73%	30%
Higher education	61	33
Organized religion	41	20
U.S. Supreme Court	50	28
The military	62	29
Major companies	55	18
Executive branch of government	41	17
The press	29	28
Congress	42	18
Organized labor	22	10
Advertising agencies	21	—
Average	45	21

Source: Harris and Associates, 1979.

a tax cut it would benefit people unlike themselves (*Public Opinion,* May-June 1978, p. 22), while there was nearly a four-fold increase in the proportion of people—from 9 perfent in 1966 to 35 percent in 1977 (*Public Opinion,* May-June 1978, p. 23)—who felt left out of the things going on around them.

It is little wonder that today's college students reflect

this growing pessimism about the nation and its institutions. Two out of three entered adolescence[1] between the time Lyndon Johnson's dream of a Great Society faded and Gerald Ford promised to end a long national nightmare. During this period, national leaders and youth heroes were assassinated, cities were burned, an unpopular war was fought in Asia, a Democratic convention brought rioting, protesting students were killed by National Guardsmen, intelligence agencies spied on citizens, a president and a vice-president resigned from office for illegal activities, and cabinet officers were tried in the courts for crimes. In 1979, when students at 26 colleges and universities were asked what historical and political events had most influenced their views, it was these they cited most frequently. This is shown in Table 4. For three out of four of those who responded, the influence of these events was negative (Carnegie Study, 1979). Few remembered the Kennedy or the early Johnson years, but then again the average freshman was only one or two years old when John Kennedy died.

These events had a greater impact on this generation than they might have for others.[2] Part of the reason is that the protective and potentially moderating social institutions most intimately associated with the development of optimism and trust in youth—the family and the schools—waned in influence during this period (see Erikson, 1963, and Tiger, 1979). In contrast, the influence of the mass media, and in particular of television, increased dramatically.

During the 1960s and early 1970s, families continued to decrease in size, less with respect to children than in terms of the number of adults. The extended family, consisting of grandparents, uncles, aunts, and cousins living in close prox-

[1]The critical importance of adolescence in human development has been demonstrated in the work of Piaget in intelligence, Kohlberg in morals, and Adelson and O'Neil in politics.

[2]Major social changes like the depression and world wars had a direct and profound impact on the generations that experienced them (Cain, 1970; Elder, 1974), but the events described here are not of this type. Watergate and Vietnam did not touch the lives of as many Americans as deeply as the poverty of the depression or the experience of fighting in or losing a brother or father to World War II.

Table 4. Events most influencing college students

Event	Percent of sample citing
Draft—Vietnam	28%
Watergate	24
Civil rights	15
Assassinations	11
1960s protest	8
Growing up in another country	6
Parents	6
Women's movement	4
Mideast	4
Energy crisis	4

Note: No other responses were offered by more than a handful of students. Multiple responses were permitted.
Source: Carnegie Study, 1979.

imity, became less common (Bronfenbrenner, 1970, p. 99), and the shelter accorded the child by the nuclear family decreased. The number of single-parent families skyrocketed. Between 1967 and 1977, the U.S. divorce rate doubled (Nordheimer, 1977, p. 7). Today, about one out of every three marriages ends in divorce. In a study of "Marital Disruption and the Lives of Children," Bane estimated: "in the 1970s, between 20 percent and 30 percent of all children under 18 will experience the divorce of their parents; an additional 3 percent to 5 percent can be expected to be affected by an annulment or long-term separation; and about 9 percent will lose one or both parents by death. Thus, between 32 percent and 44 percent will be involved in marital disruption. Another 2 percent will spend a substantial period of time in a single-parent home with a never married mother, bringing the total to between 34 percent and 46 percent" (Keniston and others, 1977, p. 229). By 1976, 18 percent of all college students reported having lived in a home without their father or mother during most of high school (Carnegie Surveys, 1976). The amount of time parents spent outside the family also increased. In 1969, 55 percent of the mothers of college freshmen were full-time housewives. By 1979, the proportion declined to 29 percent (ACE/UCLA Surveys, 1969, 1979). After a 25-year study, Uri Bronfenbrenner (1970, p. 102) reported that "American parents do not spend as much time with their children as they used to." In fact, by 1972 some 71 percent of 214,000 college-educated adults surveyed by *Better Homes and Gardens* (1972) believed that family life in America was in trouble. As a result of these changes, the family acts less as an isolating or protective cocoon today than it once did and young people today experience contact with the real world at an earlier age.

The schools have changed in a like manner. Where they once provided socialization for the adult world, they now provide an experience more akin to life in the adult world. In 1977, the U.S. Office of Education reported that school vandalism cost more than half a billion dollars a year, the highest level ever and a sum equivalent to the nation's annual textbook expenditures ("Vandals Are Keeping Busy," 1977). Moreover, a U.S. Senate subcommittee on juvenile delinquency found that "between 1970 and 1973 for the nation as a whole . . . assaults on teachers rose by 77.4 percent (for a total of 70,000 serious assaults annually by 1973), assaults on students by 85.3 percent, robberies by 36.7 percent, rapes and attempted rapes by 40.1 percent, homicides by 18 percent, and weapons confiscations by 54.4 percent" (DeCecco and Richards, 1975, p. 51). Therefore it comes as no surprise that 84 percent of Americans—a 19 percentage point increase since 1954—think that discipline in the schools is inadequate.

In the past ten to fifteen years, academic standards also have changed. This was the conclusion of a blue-ribbon panel on the decline of student college board scores, chaired by Willard Wirtz. "Absenteeism (15 percent is common, 20–25 percent is not unusual) formerly considered intolerable is now condoned. An A or B means a good deal less than it used to. Promotion from one grade to another has become almost automatic. Homework has apparently been cut about in half" (Advisory Panel on the Scholastic Aptitude Test Score Decline, 1977, pp. 28–29). Between 1969 and 1978, the percentage of college freshmen reporting high school grades of A— or better almost doubled (12.5 percent to 23.3 percent), while that of freshmen with averages of C or less dropped by a factor of three (23.7 percent to 7.1 percent) (ACE/UCLA Surveys, 1969, 1979). At the same time, the curriculum of the schools became more eclectic, individualized, and relevant or worldly (Levine, 1978). In short, the traditional conception of the school as an educational haven and moratorium for the young from the vicissitudes of the adult world is inaccurate. At worst, schools force youngsters to contend with the terrors of the adult world at an earlier age than many did in the past. At best, the decline in academic standards requires of young people less commitment to school and provides more time for unplanned activities—frequently television—in less sheltered environments.

Where the schools and the family failed to counteract the social experience of the 1960s, television appears to have reinforced it. Between 1950 and 1974, television spread from 13.6 percent of American households to 98 percent (Bureau of the Census, 1975). The children born in the late 1950s and early 1960s were the first total television generation.

Young people are television's largest audience: they watch television for an average of two to four hours a day (Keniston and others, 1977, p. 51). Preschoolers spend more time in front of television sets than any other age group, averaging 20 to 54 hours a week (Advisory Panel on the Scholastic Aptitude Test Score Decline, 1977, p. 35; Winn, 1977, p. 9). By the age of sixteen, the typical youngster has watched 12,000 to 15,000 hours of television, the equivalent of 16 to 20 months of television viewing, 24 hours a day (Advisory Panel on the Scholastic Aptitude Test Score Decline, 1977, p. 35). Since the 1960s, average viewing time has increased by about an hour a day, so that television now occupies more time in children's lives than their parents or friends (Advisory Panel on the Scholastic Aptitude Test Score Decline, 1977; Keniston and others, 1977, p. 51).

And despite improvements in children's television, young people comprise a major share of the audience for adult programs. This tendency begins in the preschool years. For example, more five-year-olds were able to identify pictures of Lucille Ball than characters from "Sesame Street" or the star of another children's program, "Mister Rogers," and situation comedies were more popular among this age group than "Sesame Street" (Lyle and Hoffman, 1976, pp. 51, 54–55). Television is the way current college students learned about Vietnam, Watergate, the assassinations of the 1960s, and the other social events they believe to be so important in their lives. They watched them in their living rooms, when the actual events occurred or only hours later. As one Trinity College student noted, "The Vietnam War I remember all of my life. As a kid it was on TV every night " (Carnegie Study, 1979). For the adolescents of the late 1960s, television was two to six times more influential in learning about the Vietnam War than their churches, their families, their schools, or even their friends (Hollander, 1971).

Added to this is the fact that the content of what children watched between 1960 and 1974 changed appreciably. In 1960, the most watched portrayal of American family life was "Father Knows Best."

> It was set in the typical Midwestern community of Springfield, where Jim Anderson was an agent for the General Insurance Company. Every evening he would come home from work, take off his sports jacket, put on his comfortable sweater, and deal with the everyday problems of a growing family. Both Jim and his wife Margaret were portrayed as thoughtful, responsible adults. When a family crisis arose, Jim would calm the waters with a warm smile and some sensible advice. . . .
>
> The Andersons were truly an idealized family, the sort that viewers could relate to and wish to emulate. The children went through the normal problems of growing up, including those concerning school, friends, and members of the opposite sex. They didn't always agree with their parents

and occasionally succeeded in asserting their
independence. . . .

The series became such a symbol of the "typical" American family that the U.S. Treasury Department commissioned the producers to film a
special episode to help promote the 1959 U.S. Sav-
ings Bond Drive. The story, "24 Hours in Tyrant
Land," told how the Anderson children attempted
to live for a day under a make-believe dictatorship.
Never aired on television, this special episode was
distributed to churches, schools, and civic organizations to show the importance of maintaining a
strong American democracy (Brooks and Marsh,
1979, pp. 196–197).

"Father Knows Best" and a whole host of like-minded
programs, including "Leave It to Beaver," "The Adventures
of Ozzie and Harriet," and "The Donna Reed Show," had left
the air by 1966. They were succeeded by a new breed of program, which portrayed family life in an entirely different
way. In 1971, "All in the Family" was the highest-rated television show in the United States. It remained number one
for four years and never fell lower than twelfth in national
ratings.

"All in the Family" changed the course of television
comedy. It brought a sense of harsh reality to a TV
world which previously had been populated largely
by homogenized, inoffensive characters and stories
that seemed to have been laundered before they
ever got on the air. Its chief character, Archie
Bunker, was anything but bland. A typical work-
ing-class Joe, he was uneducated, prejudiced, and
blatantly outspoken. He was constantly lambasting virtually every minority group in existence.
His views on blacks (or, as he often called them,
"jungle bunnies" or "spades"), Puerto Ricans

("spics"), Chinese ("chinks"), and any other racial or religious group not his own were clear and consistent. Archie believed in every negative racial and ethnic stereotype he had ever heard.

Unfortunately, he could never get away from the people he despised. Archie was a dock foreman for the Prendergast Tool and Die Company, and he had to work with a racially mixed group of people. Next door to his small house . . . in the Corona section of Queens, New York, lived a black family, the Jeffersons. His daughter Gloria had married a Pole. On top of it all, Archie, the bigoted archconservative, even had to share his house with his "egghead" liberal son-in-law. , . . Completing the Bunker household was Archie's slow-witted but honest and unprejudiced wife, Edith (Brooks and Marsh, 1979, p. 20).

As "Father Knows Best" had done in its time, "All in the Family" launched a wave of shows of a similar genre—"Maude" (about liberal upper-middle class suburban life), "Bridget Loves Bernie" (about ethnic and religious intermarriage), "Chico and the Man" (about white racism and Chicano culture), "The Jeffersons" (about social mobility and black racism), "One Day at a Time" (about divorce and the single-parent family), and "Good Times" (about big-city ghetto life). Rather than modeling an ideal like "Father Knows Best," these shows trotted out the real and seamier side of life. Rather than highlighting the normative side of middle-class life, they emphasized the differences among people—class, race, sex, and ethnicity, to name only a few. They also undermined the notion of the autonomous and independent nuclear family, whose members rallied to face and solve all the problems that came their way. Instead, they portrayed the family as continually under siege from the outside by such unpredictable and intractable problems as unemployment, crime, and discrimination. Internally, it was

buffeted by bouts with divorce, abortion, death, mental illness, and sexual dilemmas of all stripes.

Television also became more violent during this period.
In 1975, eight out of ten network programs and nine out of
ten children's weekend shows contained some violence—in
fact, 20 percent more violence than in 1958 (Winn, 1977, p.
76; Gerbner and Gross, 1979, p. 47). A much more critical
change involved the increased proximity of television violence to the viewer. Of the 25 highest-rated television series
in 1959-60, 14 shows could be described as violent, but only
two of these shows were concerned with the present, while
the rest, like "Wyatt Earp" and "Gunsmoke," dealt with the
American West of the past. In contrast, eleven of the top
twenty-five series in 1974-75 could be termed violent, but of
these only one was concerned with the past and ten with the
present such as "Streets of San Francisco" and "Kojak." As a
result of this shift, violence has become a thing of the here
and now, taking place in familiar settings and involving
everyday people like the police officer down the street. In
fact, the events portrayed in television fiction do not seem all
that different from the events telecast on the evening news,
which, by the way, increased from 15 minutes at dinner time
to 90 minutes an evening during this same period.

The change in the proximity of violence as well as the
new realism of television programming may contribute to the
findings of Gerbner and Gross (1979) that young people and
other heavy television watchers share a heightened sense of
insecurity and risk and exaggerated perceptions of their own
chances of being involved in real-world violence. Students at
the State University of New York College at Old Westbury
complained bitterly that television had turned them into a
generation of solitary "window watchers," "all huddled up in
their houses with fear." The full impact of television is un-
clear, but it is certain that in its very short history it has become one of the nation's principal babysitters, exposing the
young to adult issues and problems even in their preschool
years, a time once thought more appropriate for fairy tales
and enchantment.

When Dreams and Heroes Died

For college students, all these changes—in the society, in the family, in the schools, and in the media—have resulted in a sense that things are falling apart. This year's entering freshmen believe that all social institutions, from large corporations to the church, are at least somewhat immoral or dishonest, as shown in Table 5. There is nothing left to hold on to. Campus interviews at twenty-six colleges across the nation show that this feeling is strongest among the young, who have never experienced better times. One undergraduate summed up the mood by commenting simply, "Everything is bad."

To escape an inhospitable world, students, like much of the rest of the country, are turning inward. For many, the one remaining refuge is "me." Discussing the mood on their campuses in 1979, students from around the country said:

—People only care about me, me, me!
—We're just interested in staying alive.
—We're part of the me generation.
—Concerns today are not about social issues, but about me.

Table 5. What college freshmen think about the honesty and morality
of national institutions

	Percent saying considerably dishonest or immoral
Large corporations	41%
Major labor unions	41
Congress	39
President and administration	37
National news media	36
Police and law-enforcement agencies	31
Courts and justice system	24
Public schools	23
U.S. military	21
Colleges and universities	20
Churches	18

Source: Bachman and Johnston, 1979, p. 86. Reprinted from *Psychology Today* Magazine. Copyright © Ziff-Davis Publishing Company.

—People are looking out for number one.
—The me generation is not concerned with the good of society but with what's good for themselves.

In fact, during the twenty-six campus visits students at a majority of the institutions (54 percent) described their peers as concerned with themselves. Interestingly, they offered this information when asked to tell about the ways in which today's students are *not* apathetic. One senses the development of a lifeboat mentality among students. Each student is alone in a boat in a terrible storm, far from the nearest harbor. Each boat is beginning to take on water. There is but one alternative: each student must singlemindedly bail. Conditions are so bad that no one has time to care for others who may also be foundering.

Meism has been called "the third great awakening" by Tom Wolfe (1977), "the new narcissism" by Peter Marin (1975), and "psychic self-help" by Christopher Lasch (1976). In 1979, Lasch (1979) went so far as to describe American society as *The Culture of Narcissism*. We see it today on bookstands, where the shelves are lined with such popular volumes as *Looking Out for Number One* (Monsky, 1975), *Winning Through Intimidation* (Ringer, 1976), *Getting Your Share* (1976), *Pulling Your Own Strings* (Dyer, 1978), and *How You Can Profit from a Monetary Crisis* (Browne, 1974). We see it on campus, where books by Ayn Rand are seeing a revival and best-sellers include *Your Erroneous Zones* (Dyer, 1976), *The Crash of '79* (Erdman, 1976), *My Mother/Myself* (Friday, 1977), *Passages* (Sheehy, 1976), *Roots* (Haley, 1976), and *When I Say No, I Feel Guilty* (Smith, 1975). We witness it today in a burgeoning number of newly popular activities both on and off campus, such as natural foods, jogging, martial arts, Eastern religions, and transcendental meditation, and we hear it today in our daily conversations. Marin notes (1975, 45–46):

> I am . . . dining with a close friend in a New York restaurant, and as we eat our steaks and drink our brandy and smoke our fat cigars he explains to me

that the world is obviously overpopulated, and that somebody must starve, and that we, as a nation, must decide who it will be, and that it might as well be those who already suffer from protein deficiency, for they are already "useless." Or I finish a lecture to the members of the American Association for Humanistic Psychology, and a therapist rushes up to me afterward and asks me whether or not I believe in the "ethics of the lifeboat," and when I tell her that I don't know why we are in the lifeboat while others are drowning, she whispers knowingly to me: "We have a higher consciousness." Or I am invited to meet with a well-meaning California legislator who is beginning a political movement based on the therapeutic values of "authenticity" and "warmth," and he draws for me on a napkin the button he has designed: the single letter *I* on a blank white background. Or I attend a dinner sponsored by the Population Institute at the Century Plaza in Los Angeles, where Paul Ehrlich addresses a thousand well-heeled people about the "coming end of affluence," and when I leaf through a copy of his book given away for free I see that he recommends filling the cellar with food and buying a gun and relying on neither friends nor neighbors but only on oneself. Or, finally, I listen for two hours in a graduate seminar to two women therapists explaining to me how we are all entirely responsible for our destinies, and how the Jews must have wanted to be burned by the Germans, and that those who starve in the Sahel must want it to happen, and when I ask them whether there is anything we owe to others, say, to a child starving in the desert, one of them snaps at me angrily: "What can I do if a child is determined to starve?"

These are ideas that seem light-years from our visions of Camelot. Rosabeth Kanter makes clear just how far they are

from the historical ideal of community, which she calls
"utopia."

> Utopia is the imaginary society in which human-
> kind's deepest yearnings, noblest dreams, and
> highest aspirations come to fulfillment, where all
> physical, social, and spiritual forces work together
> in harmony, to permit the attainment of everything
> people find necessary and desirable. In the imag-
> ined utopia, people work and live together closely
> and cooperatively, in a social order that is self-
> created and self-chosen rather than externally im-
> posed, yet one that also operates according to a
> higher order of natural and spiritual laws. Utopia is
> held together by commitment rather than coercion,
> for in utopia what people want to do is the same as
> what they have to do; the interests of the individu-
> als are congruent with the interests of the group;
> and personal growth and freedom entail responsi-
> bility for others. Underlying the vision of utopia is
> the assumption that harmony, cooperation, and
> mutuality of interests are natural to human exis-
> tence, rather than conflict, competition, and ex-
> ploitation, which arise only in imperfect societies.
> By providing material and psychological safety and
> security, the utopian social order eliminates the
> need for divisive competition or self-serving actions
> which elevate some people to the disadvantage of
> others; it ensures instead the flowering of mutual
> responsibility and trust, to the advantage of all
> [Kanter, 1972, p. 1].

Three characteristics stand out in this definition: volun-
tary individual commitment and cooperation; congruence of
individual and group interests, whereby trust and mutual responsibility replace self-serving action, to the advantage of
all; and attainment by the individual of what he or she deems
necessary or desirable.

No known community or society has achieved this state, but there are times when societies move in this direction—periods of what can be called "community ascendancy"—and times when they move in the opposite direction—periods of "individual ascendancy." The relationship between the individual and the community is continually changing. At times when society is perceived to be moving toward the community ideal, individual ties with the community are strengthened and community is the dominant theme. In times when the society appears to be moving in the opposite direction, individual ties with the community are attenuated and the individual is dominant. An emphasis on "me" is what differentiates periods of individual ascendancy from periods of community ascendancy. The orientation of individual ascendancy is hedonistic, emphasizing the primacy of duty to one's self, while that of community ascendancy is ascetic, stressing the primacy of duty to others. Individual ascendancy is concerned principally with rights, community ascendancy with responsibilities. There is a comparable dichotomy between taking and giving. Individual ascendancy is present-oriented, focusing on the differences among people. Community ascendancy, in contrast, is future-oriented and concerned with the commonalities among people:

Individual ascendancy	*Community ascendancy*
Emphasis on duty to self	Emphasis on duty to others
Concern with rights	Concern with responsibility
Acceptance of the propriety of taking	Acceptance of the propriety of giving
Present orientation	Future orientation
Focus on the differences among people	Focus on the commonalities people share
Hedonistic	Ascetic

That today's college students have grown up or lived in an age of individual ascendancy is unmistakable. As will become increasingly evident in later chapters, its spirit pervades the nation's campuses.

Nearly 2,500 years ago, Aristotle described young men and old men in his *Rhetoric*. In attitude, today's college students resemble his old men more than the young (Lipset, 1976, p. 120).

> Young men have strong passions, and tend to gratify them indiscriminately. . . . They are hot tempered and quick tempered . . . owing to their love of honor they cannot bear being slighted and are indignant if they imagine themselves unfairly treated. . . . They love . . . money . . . very little, not having yet learnt what it means to be without it. . . . They have exalted notions, because they have not yet been humbled by life or learnt its necessary limitations . . . They would rather do noble deeds than useful ones; their lives are regulated more by moral feeling than by reasoning. . . . They think they know everything and are always quite sure about it; this, in fact, is why they overdo everything.
>
> [Old men] have lived many years; they have often been taken in, and often made mistakes; and life on the whole is a bad business. The result is that they are sure about nothing and *under-do* everything. They "think" but they never "know"; and perhaps because of their hesitation they always add a "possibly" or a "perhaps". . . . Further, their experience makes them distrustful and therefore suspicious of evil. . . . They guide their lives too much by considerations of what is useful and too little by what is noble—for the useful is what is good for oneself and the noble what is good absolutely. . . . They lack confidence in the future; partly through experience—for most things go wrong, or anyway worse than one expects. . . .

Like Aristotle's old men, today's college students live in a time when dreams and heroes have died.

3

Politics: The Legacy of Vietnam and Watergate

Government doesn't give a damn.
All politicians are crooks.
They are just in it for the money.
Nixon was like all of us, only he got caught.
Nixon was a victim, that's all.
When you come from New York, there are lots of little Watergates.
It happens all the time.
The whole thing was blown out of proportion.
I learned a good government lesson. The system worked. They were caught in the end.
I couldn't care one way or the other.
I don't trust government as far as I can throw the capitol building.

This is a representative sampling of the comments college students across the country offer about the personal effects of Watergate (Carnegie Study, 1979). For this generation, Watergate and Vietnam have defined the nature of the world. These two events have had an even larger impact on their political views than implied in the last chapter.[1] There it

[1]Arterton (1976) compared the political attitudes of third- to fifth-grade children in 1962 and in 1973 during Watergate. He found a sharp change in the perception of the presidency, as distinguished from the president—"the overbenevolent leader

was noted that, of those interviewed, 28 percent mentioned the draft or Vietnam and 24 percent cited Watergate as major influences in shaping their world views. What was not noted though were the answers of the rest of the students when they were asked why they had not mentioned either of those events. Some students said that they were too young to remember the war in Vietnam very well. For example, a freshman who responded that she only dimly remembered the events of the war remarked that, on the other hand, she could not remember a time in her youth when there was no Vietnam. But others said that the events were simply of no importance to them. The most common response to Watergate was, in effect, "Politics and politicians are like that; Nixon just got caught." They did not mention it because it did not stand out: it amounted to no more than additional confirmation about the way the world is, in government, in business, and in all other sectors of society. One student said, "Vietnam and Watergate go together. They really did something to people our age—so much, we don't even think about them anymore." A surprising number of students simply smiled when the question was asked, thinking that the interviewers were joking or the question naive.

Among some (16 percent) of those who cite Vietnam or Watergate as significant in affecting their world view, the effect of those events was positive, encouraging them to consider careers in journalism or politics, engendering a renewed appreciation of ethics, or making them feel that the

---

[of 1962 was] transformed into a malevolent leader" (p. 32). Perceptions of politicians as selfish, unintelligent, dishonest, and unlikely to keep their promises rose. Political cynicism greatly increased. In interpreting these results, it is important to realize that Arterton's sample was generally aware of Watergate and that it overwhelmingly took anti-Nixon stands, crediting television for their views more than their family or schools. A similar study by Rodgers and Lewis (1975) carried out after Arterton's research, during the Ervin Committee hearings and the House of Representatives impeachment inquiry, resulted in even more negative findings regarding the presidency in general and Nixon in particular. Incidentally, both this study and one by Hershey and Hill (1975) indicate that positive political attitudes among preadults began declining during the Vietnam period.

system works because the perpetrators of Watergate were caught. However, for the majority (52 percent), the effect was negative. In language of one sort or another, they report an estrangement from politics. Thus, between 1969 and 1979, the percentage of freshmen who considered it essential or very important to keep up with political affairs dropped from 51 percent to 38 percent (ACE/UCLA Surveys, 1969, 1979).

Being sincere in their sentiments, students did not keep up. That is the conclusion of the National Assessment of Educational Progress, a project which periodically surveys the educational attainment of nine-, thirteen-, and seventeen-year-olds across the country in 10 subject areas— one of which is politics. Between 1969 and 1976, knowledge of the political process, participation in politics, knowledge of international affairs, knowledge of the structure and function of government, political empathy or respect for others, and knowledge of constitutional rights all declined for seventeen-year-olds. Those who could explain the concept of democracy declined by 13 percentage points; those who thought they could have any influence on local government fell by 17 percentage points, and those who would report a stranger slashing car tires dropped by 7 percentage points (National Assessment of Educational Progress, 1978).

Student commitment to radical politics has decreased, too. Undergraduates are more moderate today and, as several students noted, less willing to stick their necks out. Relative to 1969, fewer students classify themselves as left of center or right of center. Most locate themselves exactly in the middle, as shown in Table 6.

On off-campus political issues, this shift has been translated into more traditionally conservative stances shown in Table 7. Today, more students are likely to advocate the death penalty, less coddling of criminals, alternatives to busing, and increased concern for majority rights. Exactly the opposite has happened with respect to campus issues, as shown in Table 8. On these topics, more students are apt to oppose censorship of student publications, bans on extremist

Table 6. Freshman political orientation: 1969–1979

	1969	*1979*
Far left	3%	2%
Liberal	30	23
Middle-of-the-road	44	58
Conservative	21	17
Far right	2	1

Source: ACE Survey, 1969, ACE/UCLA Survey, 1979.

Table 7. Student opinion on off-campus political issues

	Percent Agreeing			
	Freshmen		*All undergraduates*	
Issue	*1969*	*1979*	*1969*	*1976*
Too much concern with rights of criminals	54%	62%		
Too much concern with rights of minorities and not enough about majorities			54%	60%
Racial integration of elementary schools should be achieved even if it requires busing			46	27
Death penalty should be abolished	54	34		
In the Middle East dispute, my sympathies are with Israel			79	70

Source: Freshmen, ACE/UCLA Survey, 1969; ACE/UCLA Survey, 1979. All undergraduates, Carnegie Surveys, 1969, 1976.

speeches, institutional regulation of student behavior, and compulsory public service for students.

There is no conflict in these positions. On the campus issues, student opinions reflect an increasing interest in protecting their rights, just as on the external issues they show a lower level of concern for several of the popular causes of the 1960s. A case in point is affirmative action, particularly in

Table 8. Student opinion on campus political and minority issues

	Percent Agreeing			
	Freshmen		*All under-graduates*	
Issue	*1969*	*1979*	*1969*	*1976*
College has right to regulate student behavior off campus	20%	15%		
College officials have the right to ban persons with extreme views from speaking on campus	32	26		
Preferential treatment should not be given to disadvantaged in college admissions	41	38		
Student publications should be cleared with college officials	52	40		
Students should be required to spend a year in community service			48%	36%
Most American colleges and universities are racist whether they mean to be or not			43	27
Any special academic program for black students should be administered or controlled by black people.			44	40
More minority group undergraduates should be admitted to my college even if it means relaxing normal academic standards of admission			27	22
The normal academic requirements should be relaxed in appointing members of minority groups to the faculty of my college			24	13
Students who enter college under relaxed admission standards should be graded by the same standards as other students			—	83

Source: Freshmen, ACE/UCLA Survey, 1969, 1979. All undergraduates, Carnegie Surveys, 1969, 1976.

regard to preferential treatment for the disadvantaged in college admissions. Concern with racism on campus is down: Fewer students believe special rules should govern minority programs. Fewer undergraduates today are likely to favor the administration and control of black studies programs by blacks, the relaxation of admission standards for minority undergraduates, and the reduction of hiring standards for minority faculty. Four out of five want exactly the same standards of evaluation employed for themselves and for academically disadvantaged students admitted to college with lower test scores and grades under one affirmative action program or another (Carnegie Surveys, 1969, 1976). This is the one campus issue on which students are now less traditionally liberal than in the sixties. The rationale for the change is that preferential admissions are injurious to majority students, reducing their likelihood of being admitted to a selective college and making it more difficult for them to gain admission to highly rated professional schools in medicine, law, or business. When this issue went to the U.S. Supreme Court in the case of Bakke versus the Regents of the University of California, the majority of the nine University of California campus newspapers, including the Berkeley paper, printed editorials favoring the Bakke or anti–affirmative action position. This raised eyebrows all over the country. It should not have. As noted in the preceding chapter, increased concern for self and decreased concern for others is characteristic of a period of individual ascendancy.

Political Attitudes and Activity

Today there are more college students than steel workers, coal miners, automobile workers, needle workers, and farmers combined (White, 1975). This makes students not only one of the larger consumer groups, but also one of the potentially strongest voting blocks in the country. Passage of the twenty-sixth amendment to the U.S. Constitution on October 25, 1971 enfranchised nearly half of America's college students aged 18 to 20, who previously lacked the vote. This right has been extended to state and local elections in at least 44 states.

Prior to the change, particularly in the aftermath of the McCarthy presidential campaign, which had been propelled by an army of college student volunteers, there was speculation that eighteen-year-old suffrage would radically alter the face of national politics. This has not happened.

Part of the reason is that the vote was extended to all eighteen-year-olds, not just to the third attending institutions of higher education. Consequently, even though a majority of college students (53 percent) gave their votes to Jimmy Carter in 1976, the majority of eighteen-year-olds cast ballots for Gerald Ford (Fuller and Samuelson, 1977; Pomper, 1977). This is to say that there is enormous diversity among young people, and that diversity is more powerful in politics than any shared youth culture.

Diversity is a reality among college students as well. Campuses vary widely in political orientation. While 76 percent of the students at the University of California, Santa Cruz voted for Carter, 86 percent of the students at Brigham Young voted for Ford. Even within a single college, there are extreme differences between subgroups. For instance, at Berkeley only 28 percent of all students voted for Ford, but a majority of fraternity members favored him. When taken in aggregate, though, it is fair to say that student voters are somewhat left of the country and that there is a general tendency for them to support liberal candidates and issues (Fuller and Samuelson, 1977).

College students favor the Democratic party over the Republican party about two to one, but the number of independents—people choosing no party affiliation—is growing.[2] In contrast to other young people, who have the lowest voter registration rate (44 percent) of any age group in the country, college students register and vote in proportions comparable to the general population. This means, though, that at least 40 percent of the nation's college students, numbering some four million people, sat out the 1976 presidential election (Fuller and Samuelson, 1977).

Nonetheless, the influence of college students is being felt to some extent at the national level. Carter beat Ford by fifty-seven electoral votes. In Ohio, Pennsylvania, Texas, and

[2]It would not be surprising if the Libertarian Party, with its emphasis on individual freedom, made significant gains in the next few years among college students as well as the entire adult population.

Wisconsin, which wielded 89 of the electoral votes, students contributed significantly to Carter's victory, though it is reasonably clear that they did not provide the winning margin.

- Ohio: Carter beat Ford by only 9,300 votes, but at Ohio State University he won 50 percent of the student vote, compared to 38 percent for Ford, while he outpolled Ford 59 to 32 percent in student precincts at Kent State.
- Pennsylvania: Carter outpolled Ford by 128,000 votes, but at the University of Pittsburgh he won 56 percent of the vote, compared to 41 percent for Ford.
- Texas: Carter's margin was only 156,000 votes, but at the University of Texas and the University of Houston Carter beat Ford by 77 to 21 percent and 92 to 7 percent, respectively.
- Wisconsin: Carter beat Ford by only 34,000 votes, yet at the University of Wisconsin in Madison Carter took 56 percent of the student vote, to Ford's 30 percent (Fuller and Samuelson, 1977).

The real impact of the student vote is being felt at the state and local level. Student enrollment exceeds the incumbents' margin of victory in 91 U.S. Congressional districts in 33 states (Jacobson, 1978). One can only guess how many local or state elected positions students may control. According to college administrators, more political candidates than ever before are coming to campus to ask students for their votes. In fact, some student leaders complain that during election time "the place is crawling with candidates." It is this phenomenon that gives newly emerging student lobbies much of their strength with state legislators. It explains why these groups compile and publish individual legislator profiles, regularly engage in voter registration drives, and work so hard to overturn state barriers to student registration. And it also makes clear why at least two state lobbies can confidently claim that they have legislators who will introduce any bill they draft.

Campus interviews reveal, however, that the student

vote may be soft. Most students believe that they should vote and that voting probably makes some difference. Yet a substantial minority view their enfranchisement as a chore—a civic obligation or "hassle" they would feel guilty about neglecting. For these young people, voting has become ritualistic, and they have become marginal voters. Many are alienated from politics and share a sense that rhetoric, advertising, duplicity, and politics as usual are invincible. As one student noted, "Money talks, bullshit walks." Voting is equated with the latter. Political alienation does not mix well with voting motivated largely by recollections of civic lessons learned long ago. It seems in the future that one or the other will give way.

Aside from the work of lobbies and me-groups, which will be discussed shortly, actual participation in politics, is definitely down. The National Assessment of Educational Progress (1978) reported that, between 1969 and 1976, the proportion of seventeen-year-olds who signed a petition dropped by seven percentage points, those who wrote letters to government officials declined by seven points, and those who helped in elections dropped by nine points. Also down is the proportion of colleges with volunteer organizations for particular political candidates, such as Students for Carter/Mondale. Between 1969 and 1978, the percentage of institutions housing such groups dropped from 36 percent to 25 percent (Carnegie Surveys, 1978).

These numbers should not suggest, however, that political participation is dead. Massive volunteer efforts, like those involved in the 1968 McCarthy campaign, when 3,500 to 4,500 students trudged through the snows of New Hampshire and 8,000 worked in Wisconsin to win presidential primaries, are gone. But there are such occurrences as the party switchover at Stanford University, in which large numbers of students changed their party affiliation from Democratic to Republican to save liberal Congressman Paul McCloskey from defeat in the Republican primary. And certainly small cadres of students were active in campaigning for Republican John Anderson and Democrats Ted Kennedy and Jerry Brown in the 1980 primaries.

From Ideological Politics to Interest Group Advocacy

Hand in hand with these changes in off-campus campaigns
has come a decline in ideological politics of all types—left,
right, and center. Students for a Democratic Society (SDS),
the best-known and most visible of the 1960s campus groups,
is gone. It died with the decade of the 1960s, approximately
ten years after its creation, from factionalism—splits between old-line conventional leftists, Maoist Progressive Labor
people, the ultraradical Weathermen, women, blacks, and an
assortment of other political persuasions. Originally founded
as a liberal-populist group and a few years later supported by
the United Auto Workers, its times pulled it in a variety of
different directions simultaneously, causing the ideological
infighting that ultimately tore it apart.

Less well-known leftist organizations, such as the Spar-
tacus League, Young People's Socialist League, and Com-
munist Party, though still alive, are found on fewer campuses. This is also true of such conservative groups as Young
Americans for Freedom and the John Birch Society. More
traditional and mainstream political associations have also
lost ground, most notably the college branches of the Democratic and Republican parties, which have a shadowy pres-
ence on the nation's campuses and come alive, if at all, only
during election periods. The drop in representation for all
such groups is shown in Table 9.

These groups are being replaced, at a fast pace, by a
very different style of political organization, one which is
more compatible with the current student mood. These are
self-interest or me-oriented groups, concerned with protecting or improving the lot of a single class of people, be they
blacks, women, Latins, gays, Iranians, or New Yorkers. Some
of the groups are old and familiar, others are new, but they
all appear to be growing, as shown in Table 10.

Student government officials and campus newspaper
editors at 26 colleges describe these groups, particularly the
oldest of them—black student associations—as among the
most powerful or influential organizations at their schools.

**Table 9. Percentage of campuses with selected
ideological political groups**

	1969	*1978*
Students for a Democratic Society	16%	0%
Leftist political groups (for example, Progressive Labor Party, Young People's Socialist League, and Communist Party)	9	8
Rightist political groups (for example, Young Americans for Freedom and the John Birch Society)	10	4
College Republicans	43	28
Young Democrats	44	30
Average	24	14

Source: Carnegie Surveys, 1978.

Table 10. Percentage of institutions with selected self-interest groups

	1969	*1978*
Black groups	46%	58%
Women's groups	27	48
Latin or Chicano groups	13	22
Native American groups	6	13
Gays	2	11
Average	19	30

Source: Carnegie Surveys, 1978.

Only student government is mentioned more frequently. And remarkably, student newspapers and fraternities and sororities are cited less often, as shown in Table 11.

Self-interest groups tend to be closed in character. Whites, for example, know little about black student associations, and men are ignorant about the workings of women's groups. Self-interest groups are small in size, with a core membership generally numbering less than a score and seldom exceeding fifty on campuses of any size. However, social events such as dances and lectures can swell the ranks by hundreds or even thousands. Like the ideological political groups, self-interest associations are fragile and subject to

**Table 11. Perceptions of the most powerful or influential campus groups
by campus newspaper editors and student government officials**

	Percentage of respondents citing
Student government	60%
Afro American Association	37
Campus newspaper	33
Fraternities and sororities	26
Latin students	11
Dormitories	11
Women's group	11
Hillel	7
Athletes	7
Radio	7
Minority groups	7

Source: Carnegie Study, 1979.
Note: No other group was mentioned more than once. However, among those mentioned once were nurses, gays, daycare mothers, veterans, international students, accounting students, and various religious groups. Multiple responses were permitted.

phoenix-like appearances and disappearances with changes in leadership. Mitosis or splitting is also a problem, with the spirit of meism encouraging the formation of smaller and smaller groups. The University of Oregon, for example, has six or seven women's groups. At another institution, black women have split from the black student's association, and the science majors have left the black women's group to form a black women scientists' club.

The activities of self-interest groups are of four principal types—service, political action, education and consciousness raising, and entertainment. By way of illustration, the service activities of women's groups at twenty-six schools in which they were examined are extensive, ranging from counseling, medical assistance, and rape prevention to neighborhood support groups, daycare, and tutoring. Their on- and off-campus political activities run the gamut from litigation, lobbying, and support for political candidates to plain old-fashioned demonstrations and righteous indignation in support of such causes as daycare, the equal rights amendment, jobs, and women's recruitment. Consciousness raising, education, and entertainment overlapped, but included such tried-and-true activities as lectures, films, concerts, and school newspaper articles, as well as such novel approaches as coffee houses and women's days or weeks.

Program quality and success depend very much on the leadership, membership, and political persuasion of the individual groups, but by and large the self-interest groups have been much more visible and well financed than their size would seem to warrant. Though quite a few women's groups are inactive, student government officials and newspaper editors praise many for their political sophistication and easy access to institutional administrators. Some are described as moribund or only "a place to go and gripe" while others are credited with substantive accomplishments, such as making a campus more aware of sexism, forcing an institution to upgrade affirmative action, stopping a fraternity pornographic film festival and wet T-shirt contest, and getting an on-campus nurse practitioner hired.

Continuation of Student Protest

Gone is the din of the preceding decade's student unrest, and the relative quiet of today has inspired a wave of nostalgia pieces about the activists of yesteryear and a sheaf of obituaries and explanations for the death of student protest. But reports of its demise are premature.

It is true that, relative to the 1960s, the number and intensity of student protests has decreased. Officials at three out of every four institutions that were able to compare activity in 1969 and 1978 reported a decline. The drop has been largest among universities awarding the Ph.D., where activism has traditionally been most common (Carnegie Surveys, 1978). The proportion of students participating in demonstrations has also fallen, from 28 percent in 1969 to 19 percent in 1976 (Gallup International, 1969; Carnegie Surveys, 1976).

However, the fact that in 1976 one out of five undergraduates had taken part in a demonstration is certainly tangible proof that student unrest is far from dead. So too is a recent list in the *National On-Campus Report* (February 1979, p. 6). Tired of hearing that student protest was a thing of the past, the editors of that publication collected examples of student unrest during a ninety-day period extending from November 1978 to February 1979. Intentionally omitted from the list were highly publicized protests and protest issues such as South African investment policy and political changes in Iran and China. Included instead were the following:

- University of Alaska students and other environmentalists protested a pending off-shore oil drilling lease sale.
- Women at the Southern Illinois University-Carbondale picketed a fraternity house that displayed an "offensive" snow sculpture of a nude woman.
- A St. Louis abortion clinic filed for a court injunction to prevent continued sit-ins by a group of St. Louis University students.
- A showing of *Birth of a Nation* was protested as being "racist" at the University of Michigan.
- Antinuclear demonstrators from throughout the Southeast demonstrated against a proposed nuclear storage area at Oak Ridge, Tennessee.
- Possible violence and a threatened class-action lawsuit were avoided when angry Vanderbilt students who could not obtain tickets to sold-out basketball games were allowed to see the game via a hastily arranged closed-circuit television system.
- Several hundred University of Alabama students angrily chanted "Hell no, we won't go" when campus police attempted to clear the athletic ticket office when all Sugar Bowl tickets were sold before all had been served.
- One Northern Illinois student was arrested in a demonstration against an increase in checking account charges levied by a local bank.
- A Radford College student threw a pie in the face of the college president to protest sale by the college of 300 acres of recreation land.

- The student government of Suffolk University vowed that students and faculty would have to cross their picket lines at the start of the second semester unless their demands for a student trustee and additional funding from the office of the dean of students were met.
- East Stroudsburg, Pennsylvania students rallied against the administration's denial of 24-hour dorm visitation.
- Harvard students continued a long-running campaign against the J. P. Stevens textile company over alleged unfair labor practices.
- Chicano students at Amherst College occupied the student center for three days, demanding a larger office for their organization.
- Students rallied in an Atlanta park to protest a desegregation plan for the state's predominantly black colleges.

What is particularly interesting about this list are the issues that students were concerned about and the protest tactics that they used. These have changed significantly since the late 1960s.

There has been a sharp shift in protest issues, as shown in Table 12. In 1969, the three most frequent causes for unrest were the war in Vietnam, minority rights, and rules of student conduct. In 1978, they were student fees, institu-

Table 12. Percent of institutions experiencing student unrest over various issues, 1969–1978

	1969	1978
Vietnam	68%	—
Problems of minorities	35	12%
Campus rules of student behavior	22	11
Faculty/staff employment	12	18
ROTC/draft	10	—
Student fees/financial aid	2	20
Institutional facilities	3	19
Institutional services	3	12
Administration policies/practices	4	17

Source: Carnegie Surveys, 1978.

tional facilities, and faculty or staff hiring and firing. The emphasis has changed from primarily external issues to seemingly more me-oriented internal campus issues.

Moreover, the 1970s were characterized by a multiplicity of relatively equally popular causes for unrest, which varied from campus to campus, rather than by the one or two highly visible national issues like Vietnam and racism that characterized the 1960s. During 1978, the issue of South African divestment, which received much newspaper and television play, was responsible for protests on only 6 percent of the nation's campuses. Like all demonstrations in the 1960s and 1970s, the frequency of protest over South Africa varied according to a college's selectivity, its programs, its location, and its size. Divestment was most commonly an issue at large, highly selective, research-oriented universities in the Northeast and along the Pacific Coast. In fact, it was an issue at half of the country's most research-oriented universities (49 percent) but at virtually none of its two-year colleges.

From Disruption to Litigation and Lobbying

Changes in protest tactics have been at least as dramatic as shifts in the issues, as shown in Table 13. What stands out here is the decline in use of tactics familiar from the

Table 13. Percent of institutions experiencing various types of student protest: 1969, 1978

	1969	1978
Intentional destruction of property	12	1
Taking over of a building	15	*
Threats of violence	20	3
Strikes	14	1
Demonstrations	39	13
Petitions of redress	24	20
Refusal to pay tuition	*	*
Taking issues to court	4	6
Other (for example, lobbying, demanding hearings, educational activities)	4	27

Note: Asterisk indicates less than 1 percent.
Source: Carnegie Surveys, 1978.

sixties—building takeovers, strikes, demonstrations, and the destruction of property. What has taken its place are litigation and tactics ranging from lobbying and use of grievance procedures to educating the public and fellow students via seminars and research reports. These are activities more attuned to the current era, when students see less justification for violence, interruption of college classes, or even demonstrations on campus (Table 14). These activities are also more practical, more individually oriented, more suitable to causes lacking popular support, and less risky.

Student litigation and serious threats of lawsuits have increased on more than one-third of the nation's campuses (35 percent). Even more startling, at the most prestigious research universities, nearly three out of every four schools report increases, as shown in Table 15. In fact, student bodies at a number of institutions from coast to coast have hired staff lawyers or created legal services offices. This development has encouraged what might be called student-interest litigation. For example, at the University of Massachusetts, under the state's Freedom of Information Act, the student legal services office named all department chairpersons and deans in a suit attempting to obtain the release of student course questionnaires filled out by students and used by depart-

Table 14. Student reactions to various statements
about protest: 1969, 1976

	Percent of students agreeing[a]	
	1969	*1976*
In the U.S. today, there can be no justification for using violence to achieve political goals	45%	64%
Students who disturb the functioning of a college should be expelled or suspended	63	73
Student demonstrations have no place on a college campus	29	36

[a]Recorded for statement 1 is only strong agreement. Statements 2 and 3 included strong agreement and agreement with reservations.
Sources: Carnegie Surveys, 1969, 1976.

Table 15. Percentage of institutions reporting changes in student litigation or serious threats of litigation by Carnegie type

	Increased	Remained the same	Decreased
Research Universities I	74%	19%	6%
Research Universities II	63	23	14
Doctorate-Granting Universities I	38	44	18
Doctorate-Granting Universities II	55	28	18
Comprehensive Universities and Colleges I	43	38	20
Comprehensive Universities and Colleges II	38	46	17
Liberal Arts Colleges I	34	63	4
Liberal Arts Colleges II	36	50	15
Two-Year Colleges	24	64	13
Total	35	51	14

Source: Carnegie Surveys, 1978.

ments for evaluation purposes. The Student Litigation Organization at Pennsylvania State University filed a class-action suit seeking a refund for classes cancelled because of bad weather. And the student senate at Southern Oregon University, assisted by student governments at several other Oregon institutions, filed a suit charging that certain students given low grades had been evaluated unfairly, and had not been duly informed of the grading criteria ("Student Groups Fund Law Suits," 1979).

Such dramatic cases are increasing, but they have not been the primary focus of student suits. At the University of Minnesota, for example, such cases represent a very small percentage of the legal services provided to students. More common are landlord-tenant disputes (20 percent), consumer-related cases (20 percent), domestic relations problems (20 percent), and criminal misdemeanors (15 percent) (*National On-Campus Report,* June 1979, p. 7).

Developments in student lobbying have been at least as far-reaching as litigation. The 1970s witnessed the rise of two nationwide student lobbies—Public Interest Research Groups (PIRGs) and state student associations. PIRGs, proposed by Ralph Nader in 1970 and endorsed by President Carter in 1979, are now found at 11 percent of American colleges and universities on campuses located in twenty-five states (Carnegie Surveys, 1978). The theory behind the Public Interest Research Groups, which have more than 700,000 dues-paying undergraduate members nationwide, is that colleges and universities offer students theories of social change but provide no means for implementing them. PIRGs provide the structure and financial support through which students can step out of the classroom and work constructively at reform activities, while training themselves in areas of research, government, and simple good citizenship. The PIRG movement believes that, since students are affected by the same social problems as everyone else, they should work to improve the conditions under which they live.

State student associations, which have more than doubled in number since 1969, are found on 22 percent of the nation's campuses in 39 states (Carnegie Surveys, 1978). Since 1971, a national student lobby, now called the United States Student Association, has been active in Washington, D.C. State and national student lobbies behave just like any other lobbying group—they fight for legislation favorable to their constituents.

The activities of PIRGs and state student lobbies can best be understood by examining their work in a single state. New York has a highly visible PIRG, called NYPIRG, and a highly visible state student lobby consisting of four independent groups—the Student Association of the State University of New York (SASU), University Student Senate of the City University of New York, the Community College Student Association, and the Independent Student Coalition—of which SASU is probably the best known.

NYPIRG

The New York Public Interest Research Group (NYPIRG), created in 1972, has a budget of more than $950,000 derived in large part from student dues (an average of $4 per student) on campuses associated with the organization. There

are more than 125,000 dues-paying members. This figure
represents a recent loss of about 25,000, due principally to
declining enrollment on member campuses. By way of comparison, it could be noted that, at its peak, SDS had 6,000
dues-paying members and 30,000 locally affiliated members
nationwide. NYPIRG also receives money from foundations,
churches, corporations, and government through such programs as CETA and VISTA. Approximately two dozen campuses throughout New York state are currently associated
with the organization. There was periodic attrition, but the
number of participating campuses now appears to be growing. Each campus has its own student-elected and student-
run PIRG board. There is, in addition, a statewide board
composed of campus representatives. NYPIRG students and
professional staff hired by the local boards research and in-
vestigate social issues approved by the local boards. In one
recent year, this activity resulted in twenty-seven publications, including legislative profiles of all state senators and
assemblymen; reports on nuclear energy, young people and
jury selection, pollution of the Hudson River, abortion,
marijuana, and small claims court; and consumer guides on
telephone service, sales tax, nuclear energy, property taxes,
and medical malpractice.

The consequences of the reports have been of three
types—the drafting of legislation and lobbying on its behalf,
litigation, and public education via media reports and community organizing. Exemplary of NYPIRG's accomplishments are the following small sample:

- The New York legislature passed a truth-in-testing act actively supported by NYPIRG and a marijuana reform act
  that involved NYPIRG lobbying for decriminalization
  using the largest such campaign in New York state history.
- NYPIRG sued a New York legislator for illegal patronage
  payments to himself known as "lulus."
- NYPIRG uncovered widespread noncompliance with the
  Freedom of Information Act by state and local officials.
- NYPIRG drafted and lobbied into law legislation affecting

hearing aid sales, prescription drugs, and unit pricing, among other issues.

- NYPIRG established offices around the state to help people carry out small claims court judgments.
- NYPIRG sponsored and lobbied for several energy bills passed by the New York state legislature in 1977.
- NYPIRG documented bank disinvestments in Brooklyn, a practice known as "redlining," and brought the issue to the media and the local community.

Last year, hundreds of students participated in NYPIRG research projects. It is estimated that more than 500 received academic credit for their involvement. NYPIRG issues attract both liberal and conservative students. For instance, the chief lobbyist for marijuana decriminalization was a very straitlaced member of Young Americans for Freedom, which actively opposes the PIRG movement. Because NYPIRG is on the conservative and liberal sides of different issues, because it has no axe to grind, because it works in the open rather than behind closed doors, and because it produces quality reports, director Donald Ross believes it is taken seriously. In fact, a study by the Community Service Society showed NYPIRG to be one of the most active lobbies in Albany.

SASU

Twenty-two of the thirty-four units of the State University of New York belong to SASU. Each school pays dues of 85 cents per full-time-equivalent student, though under certain circumstances the rate is lower. SASU is run by an executive board, whose members are elected by the students at their home campuses. For their money and votes, students get a voter registration drive, in which 50,000 students signed up in a single year; services, such as block concert bookings, reduced rates for travel, and student shopping discounts; litigation on issues such as the state's definition of financial emancipation; testimony on pending legislation relevant to student interests; and a legislative program. During the past few years legislative efforts have included a coalition drive that successfully fought a tuition increase and a 10 percent reduction in state tuition grants and the passage of SASU-drafted bills mandating open meetings for all public bodies, requiring student representation on the Higher Education Services Corporation, which handles student loans and grants, and requiring SUNY trustees to hold four regional meetings each year. It is important to note, however, that most SASU bills are killed in committee.

SASU is able to accomplish much of what it does simply by providing information. It is frequently more knowledge-able about a particular issue than the legislators considering that issue. In one instance, a piece of legislation would have resulted in an unintended cut in student aid. When legis-lators were informed of this, the bill was changed to elimi-nate the loss.

SASU is well thought of by New York state legislators, both for doing its homework and for being professional. However, part of the power of the organization is that it rep-resents a sizable block of voters. It has generated 5,000 signa-tures on petition campaigns in a single day and it promotes letter-writing campaigns. More importantly, it issues press re-leases, which are printed, frequently unchanged, in campus and local newspapers around the state. SASU makes a point of publicizing candidate stands on issues relevant to students, and, as noted earlier, it also makes a point of registering stu-dents to vote. When all else has failed, SASU, alone or in coalition with other groups, has sponsored peaceful demon-strations of as many as 10,000 students in Albany and Wash-ington, D.C.

NYPIRG and SASU are two of the most successful examples of their kind. The activities of other state PIRGs and associations are similar, though their scope and ac-complishments vary widely. Deaths, rebirths, and fresh starts are not uncommon and once established, performance can be erratic. The frailties of these organizations resemble those of the me-groups, and their success depends on similar fac-tors. Competition between PIRGs and lobbies is not unusual at the campus level, nor are rivalries between different lobbies in the same state or at the national level. In fact, several colleges have lobbies of their own as well as participating in a larger state group. However, the existence of state and national networks buttresses the campus-level operation by providing for continuity, support, and, when necessary, proselytizing. Ralph Nader, for instance, in 1979 toured the nation's campuses in an effort to expand and revitalize the PIRG movement. Despite such efforts—or, perhaps more accurately, leading to such efforts—the on-campus PIRG and student association offices tend to involve small numbers of students, although there are exceptions like the PIRG at the State University of New York at Binghamton, which places a hundred students a year in internships. The low numbers seem to have little effect on results, particularly for the state lobbies. Adequate compensation for their size seems to derive from a professional staff, numbering more than a hundred at NYPIRG alone; an emphasis on off-campus activity relying heavily upon such tactics as research, lobbying, and litigation, which require only a few staff; and the potential threat of waking the slumbering student giant. Lack of participation is a more serious threat to PIRGs, which view themselves as something other than student-interest groups, since they seek to train young people in citizen participation as much as to achieve social reform. Accordingly, the work of PIRGs tends to focus less on student issues and more on community problems. For both PIRGs and state assocations, the most serious current problems appear to be recurrent gaps in leadership and restrictions imposed by states or institutions in such matters as collection of fees, political activity, and litigation. At present, the national offices of both organizations say they are healthy and growing. National PIRG, for example, recently took the leadership in organizing a very successful antinuclear march in Washington, D.C., and teach-ins nationwide are being planned for the coming year.

PIRGs and state student associations differ from the primary activist organizations of the 1960s. They are more

eclectic and use a variety of tactics, including lobbying, litigation, the media, community organizing, and demonstrations.
Many of these tactics were used much less or not at all in
the 1960s, when protest depended more on mobilizing the
masses.

Also, both organizations are more issue-oriented than
ideological in bent. It is felt by PIRGs and student associations that the absence of a party line enables them to build a
broad base of support, as individuals will work hard on the
issues they care about. The demand for an ideological commitment would turn away students who disagreed with even
a few of the organization's goals. The Republican National
Committee's College Republicans organization has found
this to be the case as well. It was able to get thousands of
students who were registered Democrats to sign petitions
supporting its stand on such issues as the tuition tax credit,
National Defense Student Loans, and students' right to work.
By orienting their activity to single issues, College Republicans can attract large numbers of students who would other-
wise be repelled by the party's political platform. For example, College Republicans reports that when President Carter,
at the height of his popularity, said he would cut National
Defense Student Loans the organization compiled an issues
and opinion package which was distributed to the press, in-
serted into the *Congressional Record,* and dispatched with petitions to colleges across the country. Within a week, College
Republicans was inundated with returned petitions.

PIRGs and state associations tend to be more pragmatic
and less idealistic than their predecessors. As a former president of the City University of New York student association
pointed out, in the 1960s students wanted "pie in the sky"
and were willing to protest even when they did not get what
they wanted. Today, students are playing to win, take whatever they can get, and then push for more.

In addition, both types of organization are better
funded and more politically sophisticated than previous student organizations. State student associations tend to rely
upon enrollment-based fees from member campuses, while

PIRGs, which use a variety of funding mechanisms, recommend the negative checkoff. That is, students are charged a refundable PIRG fee as part of their university tuition billing. They may decide not to pay this fee by placing a check mark next to a statement to that effect which accompanies the bill. This procedure works to increase funding, as an affirmative act is required to avoid the fee and as few parents notice the few dollars charged to support PIRGs among the much larger sums being requested. The PIRG and state association leaders interviewed expressed a very clear understanding of the importance of money: it pays for research, lobbying, litigation, professional staff, and a good many other activities that are much more effective than mass demonstrations or violence. As one state student lobbyist explained,"we represent voters and we don't have to drag them into the street to prove it to legislators. We know it and they know it, so it doesn't even have to be discussed. Instead, we discuss the issues and my opinion carries weight." Perhaps the best proof of this is the record of the California State College and University lobby, which boasts that no legislation that it has publicly opposed has ever been enacted.

This constellation of factors explains why student unrest seems to so many to have passed on to the great barricades in the sky. To be sure, student protest has declined significantly in recent years. But it is important to note that what protest there is is less visible. It should also be noted, first, that activism today is concerned with a multiplicity of issues rather than the one or two common concerns of yesterday; second, that the issues tend to be local, varying from campus to campus and student to student, rather than national in scope as they were in the 1960s; and third, that student protest tactics are both more individual—litigation as opposed to strikes and sit-ins—and more peaceful—lobbying as opposed to building takeovers—than they were in the sixties. Unseen activity is being confused with nonexistent activity. It is interesting to speculate whether other historical periods which have been labelled quiet or nonactivist such as the 1940s and 1950s, were, in fact, simply periods of unobserved protest.

Involvement in Institutional Governance

In the current era, yesterday's omnipresent demand for "student power" has vanished, and what seemed a preoccupation with campus governance and governance issues in the 1960s has become merely an auxiliary interest. Paradoxically, student attitudes about the role they should play in governance have changed very little between the two periods. As shown in Table 16, today's students want a slightly larger role in determining policy on admissions and faculty appointments and promotions than their predecessors, but they are willing to accept a somewhat smaller role in regulating degree requirements, course content, dormitory rules, and student discipline.

Part of the explanation for the seeming conflict is that student participation in institutional governance has increased substantially since the sixties. When asked to compare the extent of student participation in campus governance in 1969 and 1978, seven out of ten student personnel officers said that it had increased (41 percent) or at least that it had not decreased (29 percent).

In past years, committees were as integral to academic governance as gasoline to the internal combustion engine. Owing to a variety of factors, including the rise of faculty

Table 16. Roles students think they should have in selected areas of institutional governance: 1969, 1976

	Percentage of students wanting control over issues or voting power on committees	
	1969	*1976*
Undergraduate admissions policy	24%	26%
Faculty appointment and promotion	22	29
Bachelor's degree requirements	29	25
Provision and content of courses	42	32
Residence hall regulations	77	70
Student discipline	73	68

Source: Carnegie Surveys, 1969, 1976.

collective bargaining and a growing role for the states in managing higher education, the significance of committees is declining. However, it is here that students have made their greatest gains. For example, three out of four college and university presidents report that students now sit on their institution's educational policy committee, one of the most important planning bodies at any school and one which lies well beyond the pale of those matters to which student participation has been traditionally relegated. Incidentally, more than 60 percent of the presidents polled indicate that student participation in such committees has come about since 1970 (Carnegie Surveys, 1978).

In fact, visits to twenty-six college campuses revealed that students held seats on most committees at all but one of the schools. Budget and personnel committees were the two most frequent holdouts. A substantial minority of undergraduate student leaders (41 percent) were satisfied with this arrangement, while the rest pointed to student indifference, expressed generalized feelings that things could be better, or stated a preference for some such alternative as one person/ one vote that would mean student domination of the university. The latter idea was seldom offered seriously and always recognized to be pie in the sky a la mode (Carnegie Surveys, 1978). On the more humorous side, few students seemed to understand that their increased role in governance was recent or that others had fought hard for it. Several student body presidents complained bitterly or felt put upon, having to furnish their college with a never-ending supply of students to sit on "dinky committees." One threw his arms in the air and asked plaintively, "Where am I supposed to get them all? I'm no magician."

Hand in hand with increased participation in governance has come an increasingly influential role in establishing campus policy and operation. This was the opinion of over one-third (36 percent) of American college presidents. In fact, five out of six presidents believed that student government was at least as influential in 1978 as it was in 1969, if not more so (Carnegie Surveys, 1978).

However, there is little evidence of undergraduate interest in or concern with student government. Median voter turnout in student elections hovers between 26 and 30 percent (see Table 17)—approximately the same level as in 1969 (Carnegie Surveys, 1978). Joke candidates have been elected at some schools. Students at the University of Wisconsin and the University of Missouri elected student government presidents who campaigned in clown costumes, and students at the University of Georgia elected a candidate for student body president who campaigned with a bag over his head. There is nothing new in this. Frivolousness has long been a part of student government campaigns and elections. Most schools have resisted the tendency. At the University of California, San Diego, for example, a perfectly healthy German shepherd was rejected for its top job. Overall, not much seems to have changed in this respect. Some student bodies, like that at the University of Texas, have voted to end student government, while others, like Dartmouth, have reinstated it (*National On-Campus Report,* May 1978, p. 3). Several are making valiant attempts to increase the percentage of students voting. At the University of Pittsburgh, ballot booths

Table 17. Percentage of students voting in campus elections: 1978

Percentage of students voting	*Percentage of institutions*
0–5%	6%
6–10	9
11–15	11
16–20	10
21–25	9
26–30	10
31–35	6
36–40	7
41–50	8
51–60	6
61–70	5
71–80	7
81–90	2
91–100	2

Source: Carnegie Surveys, 1978.

have been set up at basketball games and voters have received free soft drinks. More modestly, at the University of Georgia, students get only coupons redeemable for small Cokes.

Nonetheless, even if undergraduates have not given student governments their ballots or sympathies, they have given them something at least as important—their money. Seventy-two percent of American colleges require students to pay a student activities fee, with a median price of $31 to $45 per year, as shown in Table 18. Collectively, this amounts to no less than $240 million each year, which is more than the annual state expenditures of Idaho, Montana, or Nevada. This kind of money can buy a great deal. It can be and it has been borrowed by institutions to tide them over during cash

Table 18. Student activity fees: 1978

Amount of fee	Percentage of institutions
$ 1–15	20%
16–30	24
31–45	16
46–60	16
61–75	8
76–90	4
91–105	3
106–120	2
121–150	5
151–180	2
181–210	*
211–250	*
251–500	*
501–1,000	*
Over 1,000	*
Nature of fee	
No fee	18%
Mandatory fee	72
Optional fee	4
Other	7

Note: Asterisk indicates less than 1 percent.
Source: Carnegie Surveys, 1978.

flow problems. It can be and it has been used to provide services that universities can no longer afford owing to shrinking budgets. It can be and it has been used to fight colleges in the courts, in the legislatures, and in the media; in some cases, student resources exceed those the institution itself can commit. Also, it can be and it has been used to achieve ends which a college desires but itself lacks the political muscle to realize. For example, the Georgia State University student lobby is working hard to bring a law school and new facilities to its campus.

That some student governments are using their funds in this way does not mean that all or most are doing so, but only that they have the potential to do so. In actuality, much of the student money, which averages more than $83,000 for every college in the country, is tied up in existing programs and projects, as are most government budgets. Flexibility is also limited by a student government's constituents. Me-groups have been particularly vigilant in halting allocations to causes they oppose. In addition, institutional rules limit discretionary spending. Eighty-two percent of American colleges prohibit the use of student funds for various activities. Political contributions and activities (at 63 percent of colleges and universities) head the list, with litigation following (at 37 percent of colleges and universities). Enforcement of these rules is a relatively simple matter, as institutions are frequently the collectors of student fees, and veto and approval power over student budgets resides in the hands of nonstudents (administrators, state bodies, faculty, trustees, or committees) at 81 percent of American colleges and universities (Carnegie Surveys, 1978). On several campuses, student body presidents complain of being forced by administrators to contribute funds for unwanted services and activities, such as athletic programs, orientation for new students, and insurance plans (Carnegie Study, 1979).

Such restrictions limit financial leverage, but they have not resulted in impotence, either on or off campus, as recent events show. Increasingly, the piper is calling the tune on campus. For example, the Florida state senate recently voted to give students, who are charged a credit-based construction fee, veto power over all building projects at the nine state universities in which their money is used. This authority previously belonged to the state regents (*National On-Campus Report,* June 1979, pp. 2, 3).

Off campus, student money is being courted and in some cases it is even being listened to. For instance, a flurry of activity resulted when student governments at several California colleges and universities considered removing their money from the Bank of America owing to its investments in racially segregated South Africa. Bank of America officials hurriedly trekked around the state to explain bank policies and urge students not to withdraw their accounts. When the bank said that it would not or could not sever its ties with South Africa, several schools, including San Jose State University, severed their ties with the bank.

In terms of potential political clout, individual student money is even more important than student activity fees. Much of this money is discretionary. Students are big consumers—and several of the student associations are acutely aware of this situation. As noted, some of SASU's activities, such as block concert bookings, student shopping discounts, and reduced rates for travel, take advantage of it and thereby increase the attractiveness and visibility of the lobby. At individual colleges, though, little seems to be happening in this regard.

There are some exceptions. The University of Toledo, for example, is starting a Student Buying Power program. Local merchants who choose to participate must pay a fee of $35 and consent to give students a stipulated discount. Participating merchants are included in a discount book distributed to all students. The Buying Power program also provides students with financial how-to advice on such topics as establishing credit and using a checking account (*National On-Campus Report,* July 1979, p. 7).

Two other schools, the University of Florida and Ball State University, have campus Better Business Bureaus. These may be the only institutions in the country that do. At

Ball State, the group services students as well as community people and deals both with typical Better Business Bureau issues and with specific student concerns, such as landlord-tenant relations. Files of tenant complaints are maintained to guide student renters. A free arbitration service is also offered. The campus bureau is staffed by a combination of students supported by federal work-study financial aid, students engaged in independent study for academic credit, and students enrolled in a course on "Marketing and Consumerism," which gives them the choice of writing a 20-page paper or working 20 hours for the Better Business Bureau. Funding consists of $750 provided by the student government—not a bad investment for a group considered a runaway success ("Student Fee Legislation," *National On-Campus Report,* June 1979, p. 2).

Better Business Bureaus and other types of me-groups are the reality of student activism in the 1970s. To be sure, the popularly perceived decline of student participation in the political system is largely real. As a group, students are more diverse and share fewer common interests, more introverted and less interested in politics. But this perceived decline is also in part an illusion due to the decreased visibility of student activism. In the 1960s Eugene McCarthy, Robert Kennedy, and Martin Luther King were national youth heroes, and the throngs attracted to them were plainly visible. Today's student activism is more likely to be tied to local people or lack "adult" leadership, and today's activism is likely to focus on "student issues" for which there are no national political leaders.

4

Education: The Great Career Competition

*"I was taught to be nice, but it doesn't make a differ-
ence in the real world."*
*"You're doing the paying. Make sure professors give
you what you want."*

- In a meeting of ten undergraduates at a well-known university, the student body president told of a fellowship
interview in which she was asked what she thought of a
course on negotiation at the Harvard Business School
which included training in "strategic lying," in light of the
university's historic role as a home of truth and a moral
sanctuary. She told the fellowship panel that the course
was a terrific idea and reminded them that the university
also has a role in vocational preparation. If learning to lie is
necessary for an occupation, she contended, the university
has a responsibility to teach it. Nine of the ten students in
the group agreed with her, and the fellowship committee
awarded her a grant.
- At another university, a group of eight undergraduates
disagreed with the popular image of today's college student as apathetic, passive, and uncaring, at least in terms of
their own institution. Several of them agreed with one
young woman who rejected the stereotype, explaining with
some pride that, while the university had an honor code,
cheating still occurred: "Because students genuinely care
about each other, they won't report cheating."

- The faculty of a required western civilization course at an Ivy League college report that their students want to be told what to do to get an A, like to be lectured to, refuse to participate in class discussions, and, unlike students in previous years, are not excited by the writings of Freud and Marx. The only reading that moves them, the professors say, is an article by Philip Slater in which it is argued that overachievement may cause chronic joylessness in America. The students are incensed at that idea.

In the course of research for this book, nearly two thousand people were asked how college students had changed since the 1960s. By far their most common answer was that undergraduates are more career-oriented today. Recall the responses of the student personnel officers discussed in Chapter One. "More career-oriented" was at the top of their list. They said so at seven out of every ten campuses surveyed. Also, it was mentioned by college presidents nearly twice as often as any other change (Carnegie Surveys, 1978).

A certain skepticism greeted these answers, a sense that those responding had blown the situation out of proportion. Career preparation has been an important part of college since Harvard opened its doors nearly 350 years ago. It seemed unreasonable that vocationalism should be so much more noticeable today. Perhaps the explanation lay in a common reading and television diet among respondents. Through that diet we all heard about a phenomenon called "the new vocationalism." Once aware of the phenomenon, we began to look for it and we saw it everywhere we looked.

This just was not the case. All of the available data indicate the people interviewed were exactly right. When undergraduates were asked in 1969 what was most essential for them to get out of college, they ranked learning to get along with people first and formulating values and goals for their lives second. Seven years later, as shown in Table 19, these aims fell to third and fourth position, being replaced by get-

Table 19. What undergraduates feel is essential to get from a college education: 1969, 1976

1969	Percent of undergraduates saying essential
Learning to get along with people	76%
Formulating the values and goals for my life	71
Detailed grasp of a special field	62
Training and skills for an occupation	59
Well-rounded general education	57
1976	
Detailed grasp of a special field	68%
Training and skills for an occupation	67
Learning to get along with people	66
Formulating the values and goals for my life	62
Well-rounded general education	57
Change between 1969 and 1976	
Training and skills for an occupation	+8%
Detailed grasp of a special field	+6
Well-rounded general education	0
Formulating the values and goals of my life	−9
Learning to get along with people	−10

Source: Carnegie Surveys, 1969, 1976.

ting a detailed grasp of a special field and obtaining training and skills for an occupation.

Top among the reasons freshmen give for attending college is to get a better job. Three-quarters list this as a rationale (ACE/UCLA Survey, 1979). More than eight in ten undergraduates say they are extremely or somewhat interested in having a credit-bearing apprenticeship, internship, or job during college. If there are still students who come to school to find themselves, rather than jobs, they are keeping a low profile. The vast majority of undergraduates (85 percent) report that they are attending college with a specific career in mind (Carnegie Surveys, 1976), and that career is firmly in mind because fewer freshmen now expect to change their job plans (12 percent in 1979 versus 17 percent in 1969) or their major area of specialized college study (12 percent in 1979 versus 16 percent in 1969).[1] Despite this determination to stick to a chosen course, college is an iffy proposition for many dependent in large measure on future jobs. Nearly half (46 percent) of all students would drop out of college if they thought it was not helping their job chances, and more than a third (38 percent) would leave college immediately if they could get the same job now as after graduation. The fact of the matter is that less than a quarter (24 percent) of all undergraduates can say that they are not worried about their postcollege job prospects.

Effects of Vocational Concern

The single most obvious result of this emerging "vocomania" is a change in student enrollment patterns. Vocational fields are drawing students in great numbers. The big gainers are business, the health professions, biology (as the gateway to medical school), agriculture, and other technical fields. Business ranks first, being the subject in which nearly a quarter of all freshmen intend to major. This represents a 50 percent increase relative to 1969. The big losers have been the fields where occupational opportunities are limited— education, the humanities, and several of the social sciences. This is shown in Tables 20 and 21. A few months ago, an administrator at a highly regarded women's liberal arts college called to inquire sheepishly what schools "like us" were doing to become more vocationally attractive.

Having chosen more career-oriented subjects, students are also spending more time studying them. The typical college curriculum is divided into three parts—the major, which has been described here as increasingly career-oriented; electives, which students can use to study any subject they wish; and general education, which has traditionally been the least overtly vocational portion of an undergraduate education, emphasizing instead a broad range of

[1] In both years, student expectations deviated widely from reality. Almost half of all undergraduates change their major during college, and career plans alter even more often.

Table 20. Areas of concentration among undergraduates: 1969, 1978

	Percentage choosing		Direction of change
	1969	*1978*	
Agriculture	2%	3%	+
Biological science	3	5	+
Business	16	24	+
Education	11	8	−
Engineering	10	10	0
English	4	1	−
Fine Arts	9	7	−
Health professions	6	9	+
History, political science	6	3	−
Humanities (other)	4	1	−
Math or statistics	4	1	−
Physical science	3	2	−
Psychology, sociology, & anthropology	9	3	−
Other fields (technical)	4	8	+
Other fields (nontechnical)	2	2	0
Undecided	2	—	

Source: ACE/UCLA Surveys, 1969, 1979.

skills and knowledge thought to be needed by all liberally educated people. A number of scholars, including Daniel Bell, believe that one of the prime rationales for general education is contraspecialization, providing an antidote of sorts to major study. Many undergraduates seem to disagree. Compared to the 1960s, students have limited the amount of time they spend on general education and use their electives to increase the number of courses in the major. Between 1967 and 1974, the proportion of credits that students were taking in their area of concentration increased from 44 percent to 58 percent (Blackburn and others, 1976). By 1976, one out of every seven students was completing the requirements of two majors (Carnegie Surveys, 1976). At the same time, general education was reduced by more than a fifth (22 percent) (Blackburn and others, 1976). If there were no requirements, the situation would be even more lopsided, as 41 percent of college students feel that current degree require-

Table 21. Bachelor's degrees awarded by field of study: 1964–65, 1970–71, 1974–75

	Percent of degrees awarded			
Subject	1964–65	1970–71	1974–75	Direction of change
Education	23	21	16	−
Social science	16	19	13	−
Business	13	14	17	+
Letters	9	9	5	−
Engineering	8	6	5	−
Biological science	5	4	6	+
Mathematics	4	3	2	−
Physical science	4	3	2	−
Fine and applied arts	4	4	5	+
Health professions	3	3	6	+
Psychology	3	5	5	+
Foreign languages	3	2	2	−
Agriculture	2	2	2	0
Communications	<1	1	3	+
Architecture	<1	<1	1	0
Public affairs and service	<1	1	4	+
Library science	<1	<1	<1	0
Computers	0	<1	<1	+

Source: American Council on Education. *A Fact Book on Higher Education.* Washington, D. C., 1977; National Center for Education Statistics; *Bulletin 79-382.* Washington, D. C.: National Center for Education Statistics, 1976.

ments restrict them from taking as many courses in their major as they would like (Carnegie Surveys, 1976).

The humanities (literature, history, classics, art, and language)—long a symbol for general education—have suffered most from this loss of favor. For a sizeable minority of undergraduates, they are the epitome of nonutilitarian education. At least one out of every three students believes that the humanities are of value only to students planning to teach (33 percent); that they are irrelevant to the student's own interests (33 percent); and more practically, that they are useless in preparing for a job (32 percent) (Carnegie Surveys, 1976).

In eclipse as well are many of the ballyhooed educational experiments of the 1960s. The philosophy which guided them—a student-centered curriculum concerned with personal development and socially relevant studies—is out of vogue. The most exciting colleges of a few years ago, such as Hampshire and the University of California Santa Cruz campus, are finding it more difficult to attract students, particularly those with top academic credentials, and a number of widely publicized innovative subunits within larger institutions, such as Montieth College at Wayne State University, have closed their doors.

A variety of educational decisions have been made in the name of the job market and the economy. Students have quit school, students have returned, and students have stayed on longer than anticipated. Some have changed majors; others have added a vocationally advantageous second major or minor. Some undergraduates have decided to go on to graduate school and others have decided not to. All this is being done for a better position in the career sweepstakes, as shown in Table 22.

The increased vocationalism should probably not have come as a surprise. Today's students are just turning the corner on a decade that brought unchecked inflation, three recessions, and intermittent crises of unemployment. Anec-

Table 22. Educational changes undergraduates report making primarily in response to the job market or state of the economy

	Percentage responding yes
Decided to go to graduate or professional school	28%
Returned to school to get further training	23
Took technical or work-related courses	20
Considered quitting college altogether	17
Took a second major or a minor	17
Changed my major	13
Decided to stay in school an extra year	13
Decided not to go to graduate school	11
Returned to school because I couldn't find a suitable job	9

Source: Carnegie Surveys, 1976.

dotes about college graduates working as taxi drivers became common a few years ago. The value of a college degree was said by some to be declining, and the likelihood of underemployment for college graduates was reported to be growing. Despite the objective reality of an improved marketplace today for students to sell their job skills, the experiences of the recent past are very much alive and their influence continues to ripple through higher education.

Impact of Competition

Competition, the war of each against all, is one obvious result. To be sure, students who choose popular preprofessional fields, like the now burgeoning prelaw and premedical courses favored by 20 percent of the freshmen in 1979, must do very well if they are to win a place in oversubscribed and highly selective graduate schools (Bachman and Johnston, 1979, p. 80). Oddly enough, the same phenomenon exists in less popular, less vocational areas where one might anticipate much less career pressure. There is a feeling that to select such a major is to go out on a limb, but to do poorly or to stand undistinguished is to saw the limb off the tree. The reality of the situation is that four out of five undergraduates describe the students in their major as not only competitive but very competitive (Carnegie Surveys, 1976).

Such an environment gives rise to the lifeboat ethic discussed in Chapter Two and for many it generates a sense of desperation. Cheating and other forms of academic dishonesty, which were widely publicized in the aftermath of a mass cheating scandal at West Point, have increased at least slightly since the 1960s. Lansing Lamont (1979, p. 83) examined the situation at 12 selective institutions and estimated the rise to be between 20 and 30 percent. There has been a modest increase in the proportion of students nationwide who say that they have to cheat to get the grades they want. Research universities have been hardest hit. Here the rate has nearly doubled since 1969, as shown in Table 23.

Cheating is well documented at individual schools. A 1976 study at Stanford revealed that 30 percent of the un-

Table 23. Percentage of students reporting that "some forms of cheating are necessary to get the grades I want," by Carnegie typology: 1969, 1976

	1969	*1976*
Research Universities I	5.8	9.4
Research Universities II	5.3	10.5
Doctorate-Granting Universities I	6.4	7.5
Doctorate-Granting Universities II	7.8	11.2
Comprehensive Universities and Colleges I	9.0	11.1
Comprehensive Universities and Colleges II	10.6	10.6
Liberal Arts Colleges I	3.9	6.0
Liberal Arts Colleges II	8.1	7.9
Two-Year Institutions	7.8	6.5
Average	7.5	8.8

Note: The Carnegie typology is described in Appendix B.
Source: Carnegie Surveys, 1969, 1976.

dergraduates had cheated at least once. A poll at Amherst in 1974 found that 43 percent of the students surveyed had cheated on an examination or paper (Peterson, 1974, p. 1). At Johns Hopkins, which had an honor code, 30 percent of the undergraduates reported that they had cheated in one way or another by their senior year ("Johns Hopkins Scraps Honor Code," 1975, p. 2). Surveys at Dartmouth College and the University of Michigan showed that between 50 and 60 percent of students had violated the honor code at least once. Again at Stanford, the proportion of students who believed that cheating was never justified dropped from three out of four to one out of two between 1961 and 1976 (Lamont, 1979, p. 3). By and large, students have been unwilling to blow the whistle on dishonest peers. For example, a survey at the University of California, Davis, found that 75 percent of the respondents would not report a student they observed cheating (Bow, 1975, p. D-5).

Lansing Lamont (1979, p. 71) has described in sad detail the practices behind these numbers.

Students at Columbia used gum wrappers. Dartmouth men favored the "flying wedge." A group of Harvard students employed their scientific skills to devise a master code so as to obtain the answers to their physics exams in advance. At Princeton one undergraduate stole a set of completed exams with grade sheets from his chemistry professor's office; a Stanford junior led classmates to a cubbyhole in the exam hall where he had stashed copies of purloined answers to an upcoming test in sociology. All across the campuses, the sting was on. Students under pressure burglarized, plagiarized, sabotaged one another's lab experiments, trafficked in phony term papers, colluded on assignments, or furtively copied from others on exams. They sneaked homemade "cribs" into class in their shirts and socks, used mirrors, the backs of desks, watchstraps, even their bare arms as cheating implements. Some resorted to "dry-labbing," faking the results of experiments on paper; others slipped through exams, using pocket-size tape recorders with earphones to play back lecture notes or vital formulas. "If I'm in an exam, and I can get a glimpse of the other guy's paper, I'll do it," said a clean-cut-looking University of Michigan senior. "But that's not cheating, really. It's just a natural impulse."

Besides cheating, other forms of academic dishonesty have been used as a hedge against competition. Being the sole possessor of needed library materials or being able to limit a fellow student's access to necessary books and journals is one advantage. Today the theft and destruction of library books is a problem on most campuses (Carnegie Council on Policy Studies in Higher Education, 1979, pp. 11–12):

a . . . national survey of college and university libraries found that mutilation of periodicals was a serious problem at 80 percent of the institutions studied. . . . With regard to books, a 1976 inventory at the Claremont Colleges found 15,000 volumes had been stolen over the last 20 years. At the University of Maryland more than 30,000 books were missing. . . . In 1976, Princeton University found that articles on aspirin and its derivatives were ripped out of more than 100 journals. And colleges and universities throughout the country have found that Winslow Homer prints have been razored out of nineteenth-century journals. . . . The undergraduate libraries at the University of California, Berkeley; Northwestern University; and University of Washington report annual book loss rates of between 4 and 5 percent of their holdings. At Berkeley, 12 percent of the 150,000 volume undergraduate collection was lost in three years with an average replacement cost of $10 plus processing cost per book. As a consequence, 10 percent of the library's annual budget was used for book replacement. And the editors of *Library Scene* estimate the national replacement cost of college and university libraries to be no less than $63.7 million plus processing each year if only 1 percent of library collections are lost per year.

One wonders if such acts do not at least in part reflect the social events that students have witnessed. Recall the undergraduates who said about Watergate that "It happens all the time" and that "Nixon was like all of us, only he got caught." When it comes to academic dishonesty, how many students believe that everyone else does it and that they would be fools not to?

Ambivalence Over Grades

The payoff from cheating is grades. Students harbor a curious ambivalence about them, as Table 24 shows. Only one out of eight students claims not to care about grades (Carnegie Surveys, 1976), but cynicism about them is high, and the pressure to earn them is enormous. A majority of under-

Table 24. Student attitudes about grades

	Percentage of undergraduates agreeing
I am not doing as well, academically, as I would like	58%
I feel I am under a great deal of pressure to get high grades	52
It is possible to get good grades without really understanding the material	61[a]
My grades understate the true quality of my work	59[b]
It is difficult both to get good grades and really learn something	34
I don't care what grades I get	11

[a]By content, only 44 percent of undergraduates expressed this opinion in 1969.
[b]This item was answered by juniors and seniors only.
Source: Carnegie Surveys, 1976.

graduates say that they are not doing as well academically as they would like; that they are under a great deal of pressure to get high grades; that it is possible to get good grades without understanding the material in their courses; and that their grades understate the true quality of their work. In addition, one out of every three believes that it is difficult both to get good grades and really learn something (Carnegie Surveys, 1976.)

It seems contradictory that students should want good grades as intensely as they do and at the same time give so little credence to the coveted article. And it goes beyond sour grapes, as students are getting high grades. The nation's campuses, like its high schools, are experiencing what has come to be called "grade inflation." Between 1969 and 1976, the proportion of students with A and B grade point averages rose from 35 to 59 percent and the proportion with averages of C or less declined from 25 to 13 percent (Carnegie Surveys; 1969, 1976), as shown in Table 25.

With such high grades it is readily apparent why there is so much cynicism and so much pressure. For all intents and purposes, grade inflation raises the true failing grade. If three out of every five students are getting As and Bs, then C

Table 25. Grades received by undergraduates: 1969, 1976

Grades	1969	1976
A+, A	2%	8%
A−	5	11
B+	11	18
B	17	22
B−	19	15
C+	23	15
C	18	10
C− or less	7	3

Note: Totals add up to more than 100 percent owing to rounding.
Source: Carnegie Surveys, 1969, 1976.

is a mark of failure. Consequently, students must get high grades merely to survive. For those planning on a selective professional school, the situation is even worse. In the course of this research, enough anecdotes about tearful premeds who begged faculty to raise a B+ to an A were heard to fill this book.

Grade inflation began in the sixties. Its origins appear to rest with the educational progressivism, or rhetoric thereof of the period, which decried grades for their inhibiting effect on learning. The war in Vietnam was another contributing factor. At the height of the war, Selective Service announced a policy of drafting college students who had grade point averages below a certain minimum. For faculty, this made every C grade a possible death sentence.

Though the war is over and much of the rhetoric is out of fashion, grade inflation persists for a great many reasons, and students are helping it along by artificially hiking their grade point averages. On campuses all across the country, undergraduates are overenrolling in courses and dropping the ones in which they do poorly on the last possible drop date; taking optional pass-fail courses outside their majors and working harder in their graded major courses (according to the 1976 Carnegie Survey, 34 percent of the nation's students are engaging in this practice); changing from pass-

Source: Doyle, L. and Freding, M. in *Nutshell* 1979/80, p. 172.

fail to letter or numerical grades or vice versa after the first course exams and taking "gut" courses, "mickey mouse" courses, or courses known for their high grades (Carnegie Council on Policy Studies in Higher Education, 1979, p. 13). Almost half (43 percent) of all undergraduates believe that many of the successful students at their college make it by "beating the system," rather than by studying (Carnegie Surveys, 1976).

This may explain why three out of five college students believe that their grades underrate the quality of the course work they produce. In view of grade inflation, this is, of course, impossible. It would be laughable if it were not frightening. For underlying this belief must surely be a misplaced sense of entitlement, a confusion of aspiration with accomplishment, and a loss of perspective about what constitutes merit. Having gotten good grades so easily for so long, the practice has been accepted as appropriate. However, there is now an increasing sense that grade inflation has failed to keep pace with the rising costs of the marketplace, where exceedingly high grades are thought necessary to obtain the most desirable jobs and postcollege training.

Declining Skills

What makes the situation even more extraordinary is that today's college students are less well prepared than their counterparts of the 1960s. Undergraduate ability in the three Rs—reading, writing, and arithmetic—has plummeted in recent years. One indication is given by declining scores on the national college admissions examinations. Between 1963 and 1979, average scores on the College Board Scholastic Aptitude Test, which is taken by more than 70 percent of all college freshmen, dropped from 478 to 427 on the verbal portion of the test and from 502 to 467 on the mathematical part of the test. There is a possible total of 800 points on each test. Similar declines were recorded on the American College Testing Program college entrance exam, which is taken by more than half of all college-bound students. As shown in Table 26, scores fell in English, math, social studies, and natural sciences.

Another indication is the National Assessment of Educational Progress surveys of seventeen-year-olds described earlier. The studies of student writing ability, which were

Table 26. Average test scores on the American College Testing Program exams: 1963–64, 1977–78

	1963–64	1977–78
English	18.7	17.4
Mathematics	19.6	16.8
Social studies	20.0	16.6
Natural science	20.6	20.4

Note: Maximum score is 36.
Source: Unpublished information from American College Testing Program.

conducted in 1969 and 1974, found a significant decline in the mean quality of student essays. Fewer were considered average, and more were rated poor. In general, the essays contained simpler vocabulary, fewer complex sentences, more run-on sentences, and a greater number of incoherent paragraphs. National Assessment studies of reading were conducted in 1971 and 1975. Over the four-year period, there was little change in overall student ability, but there was a significant decline in comprehension among women students and among students whose parents were educated beyond high school. Mathematics surveys carried out in 1973 and 1978 also registered declines both in overall math achievement and in problem-solving ability. Most students did not understand the concepts of fractions, decimals, and percents.

Students themselves provide another indication. A sizeable minority have not studied traditional high school staples. Thirty-five percent have not taken second-year algebra, 28 percent have not had even one year of a foreign language, 27 percent have not taken junior- or senior-year English, 22 percent have missed geometry, and 20 percent have not had a year of any specific science, such as biology or chemistry (Carnegie Surveys, 1976). And while more than one out of three (38 percent) feel that some elements of their undergraduate education are a wasteful repetition of material studied in high school, as many as a quarter of all college freshmen say they need remedial instruction in reading, writing, or mathematics (see Table 27). Their professors agree. At Harvard, a senior faculty member in English reported that "students show less facility in reading and do not know grammar." At Columbia University, an instructor said that students "can't write and won't read." At the University of California, Berkeley, 40 to 65 percent of the incoming freshmen take remedial writing. At Sterling College, a sectarian liberal arts school, one half of the students have difficulty with texts written at the freshmen level. At the General College at the University of Michigan, an open admissions two-year college, only 10 percent of the students are capable

**Table 27. Portion of freshmen needing
remedial work in various subjects**

English	14%
Reading	8
Mathematics	25
Social studies	4
Science	13
Foreign languages	14

Source: ACE/UCLA Survey, 1979.

of studying college algebra or trigonometry at the time of entrance.

Perhaps one vignette sums it all up. The author of a bestselling text in marketing for community colleges recently completed a tour of a dozen or more campuses where his book is in use in order to solicit recommendations for changes in a forthcoming edition. The most common advice he received was to cut theoretical discussions to a minimum, increase the concrete illustrations, add more pictures, provide transparencies for classroom discussions, and simplify the vocabulary. He was told that the chapter on moral consequences or outcomes of business was not being read.

Amid this sea of decline, what stands out as particularly incongruous is a sharp increase in the percentage of undergraduates describing themselves as intellectuals. Between 1969 and 1976, the proportion rose from 49 to 64 percent (Carnegie Surveys, 1976). This may simply be an effect of the times. During the 1960s, the term "intellectual" denoted a vegetating ivory-tower type, one more likely, in Eldridge Cleaver's terms, to be part of the problem than part of the solution. Or it could be a reflection of the increasing amount of work that students are putting into their courses. Relative to the last decade, slightly more undergraduates, now four out of five, say that they work very hard at their studies. There may be a temptation to equate long hours at academic assignments with being an intellectual, but that, of course, overlooks motivation and confuses quality with quantity.

Consumer Satisfaction

On the face of it, the poverty of undergraduate preparation, the race for jobs, the competitive atmosphere on campus, and the pressure for grades would seem to make college a fairly dreadful experience for today's students. Not so. They are more satisfied with college than the students of the sixties, who, by the way, were extremely satisfied. In fact, a majority of the undergraduates of the 1970s report being satisfied with college in general, with their majors, with their teaching, and—surprise of surprises—even with the mechanics of grading (see Table 28). When asked whether they had gotten what they wanted out of college, students, with very rare exception, answered "Yes, quite definitely!"

Today's students are more traditional in academic values than the undergraduates of a decade ago. There is less interest in seeing things change. The much-heard demands of the 1960s for greater relevance, an end to grading and requirements, and more attention to student emotional growth are less popular among students now. Fewer believe that less emphasis should be placed on specialized training and more on a broad liberal education or that the effectiveness of teaching rather than research should be the primary criterion for faculty promotion, as shown in Table 29.

This by no means implies a new age of tranquility in the academic kingdom. When undergraduates were asked what advice they would give a high school senior planning to attend college, consumer advice topped their list, advice such

Table 28. College student satisfaction

	Percent satisfied
Your college overall	71%[a]
Your major overall	77
Your teaching at college	72
Your college's methods of grading and evaluation	57

[a]In 1969, 66 percent said they were satisfied.
Source: Carnegie Surveys, 1976.

Table 29. Student opinions on various educational practices: 1969, 1976

	Percent agreeing	
	1969	*1976*
Much of what is taught at my college is irrelevant to what is going on in the outside world.	43%	29%
Undergraduate education would be improved if course work were more relevant to contemporary life and problems.[a]	49	33
Undergraduate education would be improved if grades were abolished.	57	33
Undergraduate education would be improved if all courses were elective.	53	35
Undergraduate education would be improved if more attention were paid to the emotional growth of students.	83	74
Undergraduate education would be improved if there were less emphasis on specialized training and more on broad liberal education.	40	31
Teaching effectiveness, not publications, should be the primary criterion for promotion of faculty.[a]	66	57

[a]This includes only those people answering "strongly agree." All other items include "strongly agree" as well as "agree with reservations."
Source: Carnegie Surveys, 1969, 1976.

as "You're doing the paying; make sure professors give you what you want." And there is no reason to believe that this tendency will decline in the next few years.

Consumerism in higher education is probably as old as higher education itself. Mass complaints have been with us for more than 200 years—since at least 1766, when Harvard students walked out of the college dining hall before giving prayers of thanks because their breakfast butter was putrid. The students, whose previous complaints about butter had been greeted with punishment for insubordination, proceeded to give three cheers in Harvard Yard and breakfasted in town. Unfortunately for them, their act was considered treason against the sovereign. Neither a student petition of explanation and redress nor the fact that faculty investigators found the butter inedible was considered sufficient justification for the deed. The students were suspended, pending the receipt of a note of apology and promises that, for the rest of their tenure at the college, they would be on their best behavior. The first letter of regret the students drafted was rejected by the college president as too equivocal. The second was accepted, and happily so for the students, as mass expulsions in those years were not uncommon.

Today's student consumerism is probably closer in origin and philosophy to a mid-1960s book, *Unsafe at Any Speed,* by a young lawyer named Ralph Nader. When published, the book was read with mild interest and surprise on college campuses, but a decade and a half later its message is being taken seriously and being applied not only to industrial and environmental abuses but to complaints about colleges and universities themselves. The current consumer movement represents something more than an updating of the Harvard student complaint or even a proliferation of such events. It has five basic characteristics:

- Consumerism is a philosophy of governance. It is concerned with student rights versus college rights. In contrast, the 1766 Harvard students addressed themselves to resolving one specific problem, rather than to defining, establishing, and defending their general rights.
- Consumerism is premised on a buyer-seller relationship between the student and the college. It assumes that the marketplace is currently governed by a philosophy of caveat emptor—let the buyer beware. Until very recently, and as implied in the account of the butter rebellion, the relationship between student and college was modeled on the relation between child and parent. The college acted in loco parentis; that is, the administrators and faculty governed student behavior and lives in place of parents.
- Consumerism is active as well as reactive. It aims to improve the lot of students by securing for them the four primary rights advocated by President Kennedy in

1962—the right to be informed, the right to choice, the right to be heard, and the right to safety. But when necessary, it seeks after the fact to remedy wrongs done to students as the butter rebels sought to do.

- Consumerism seeks rights and remedies off campus as well as on campus. The court of last resort for the Harvard students was their college. Today's student can turn to state government, the federal government, accrediting associations, and even to public opinion if a problem cannot be resolved on campus. As a consequence, an increasing number of college problems are being resolved off campus.
- Consumerism is concerned with the rights and remedies of individuals as well as those of the majority. Where a mass protest by the butter rebels was needed before the quality or lack thereof in their butter could be examined, students today have a variety of avenues for seeking satisfaction on and off campus, even for an unpopular cause.

The rapid and dramatic emergence of consumerism in higher education is a consequence of the changing relationship between students and their colleges, as well as the prominence of consumerism in other sectors of society. There exists a dynamic equilibrium or state of changing balance in the relationship between students, institutions of higher education, and a historically silent third partner, social policy, as articulated in the laws enacted by the government and the opinions of the public.

At the time of the Harvard butter rebellion, students wielded little power over colleges other than deciding whether to attend or not. By contrast, the college was quite powerful, having parental authority over the students. And social policy, if at all concerned with the small world of higher education, was foursquare behind the college, since the students were guilty of a treasonous offense.

Over the years, the alignment of the three forces has periodically shifted. But never has the change in the relationship been greater than in recent years. Since World War II, social policy has occupied a much more central position in the interaction between colleges and students than it did at the time of the butter rebellion, in large measure as a consequence of government's growing investment in institutions of higher education and its increasing role in student financial aid. Of late, however, the student's hand has been fundamentally strengthened relative to both colleges and agencies or organs of social policy, and at the same time the power of the college over students has declined, as has social policy's support of higher education.

Eight factors contribute to the new student position; some of them have already been mentioned.

- The eighteen-year-old vote and the rise of student lobbies means more political clout for students.
- The conclusion of the post–World War II era of growth and the onset of steady-state, hard economic and demographic times for colleges have produced an educational marketplace that favors the buyer (students), in contrast to the growth years, which favored the seller (institutions). The change both in the marketplace and in the current economic situation has encouraged students and their parents to demand more from colleges for their money.
- Financial aid programs have been increasingly targeted at students rather than institutions, which strengthens the hand of the user of educational services to the detriment of the supplier. Moreover, high default rates on federally guaranteed student loans have increased the U.S. government's interest in consumer problems.
- Relative to the 1960s, students have greater access to university officers and more opportunities to participate in institutional governance. Consequently, students are generally more knowledgeable about institutional affairs. A glance at current student newspapers and those of years past bears this out.
- The growth in enrollments of nontraditional students, who are older, married, and employed, means that more students have competing demands outside of college and

that students must be more selective in their commitment of limited discretionary time and money.

- Students are more self-interested today.
- Public schools are more permissive. Rising absenteeism and grades are coupled with declining basic skills and discipline. Consequently, there is a greater inclination on the part of some students to produce less and demand more.
- Owing to the expansion of course offerings and the reduction of requirements at many colleges during the 1960s, institutions of higher education frequently have been portrayed as educational "supermarkets" and their students, by analogy, as educational "consumers."

The less powerful position of the college relative both to students and to social policy results from the following six factors:

- Higher education today is lower in public confidence than it was in the mid-1960s, owing in part to student unrest in the latter years of that decade, owing in part to the increased priority of other social concerns, such as health and jobs, and owing in part to a general national decline in confidence in all public institutions associated with Watergate. A 1979 Harris poll found a nearly 50 percent decline in public confidence in the leaders of higher education over the last 12 years. In 1966, 61 percent of the Harris sample expressed "a great deal of confidence" in the leaders. Today, only 33 percent do (Harris and Associates, 1979).
- The doctrine of in loco parentis is moribund on most campuses. Long recognized in practice, the doctrine was officially stated by a Kentucky court in the 1913 case of Gott versus Berea and it was reaffirmed in several subsequent decisions. In loco parentis died slowly. The first telling wound was dealt by the G.I. Bill of 1944, which brought veterans who would not and could not reasonably be treated as children onto campus. A mortal wound was

struck as the result of a series of court cases, beginning
with Dixon versus Alabama State Board of Education in
1961, which affirmed certain basic student rights inconsis-
tent with the notion of in loco parentis, and ending with
Goldberg versus the Regents of the University of California in 1967, which finally struck down the doctrine.

- In 1974 and 1975, the *Boston Globe,* the *Washington Post,* and
the *Chicago Tribune* each ran one or more articles revealing
gross student mistreatment by postsecondary proprietary
institutions; misleading advertising, low-quality programs,
inadequate facilities, and a variety of other abusive practices were involved. At least one of the articles was reprinted in the *Congressional Record,* and hearings were sub-
sequently held. As part of the postsecondary community,
colleges and universities have been subject to much of the
resulting governmental action, and perhaps to more
critical public scrutiny as well.

- With the enormous expansion of college enrollments,
higher education acts less as a screening device than it once
did. Consequently, college-trained people are not automat-
ically accorded the same status as their predecessors of decades past, nor do all receive the best jobs available in the
society or the greatest share of society's material rewards.
The fact that college is available to more of the public
makes it appear increasingly less special—more like
Woolworth's than Tiffany's. Though many students think
they are still shopping at Tiffany's, they no longer leave
college with precious jewels; as a result, they feel that college is doing its job less well. The popularization of higher
education has removed some of the mystique from college
and made it vulnerable in a way it was not previously to
precisely the same level of criticism as any other social
institution.

- The widely publicized decline of student basic skills has
made the public less satisfied with its schools at all levels,
and social policy favors a reduction in school autonomy
and increased public accountability.

- Colleges today are admitting students who are more diverse in background and ability than in the past. These students are demanding a greater variety of services from colleges, some of them conflicting, such as the simultaneous demand for more and less compensatory education. As a result, not all of the services are being provided, and colleges are subject to criticism both for their omissions and for their additions.

The phenomenon of consumerism is a direct result of these changes in colleges and students. In a dynamic equilibrium there is a stable relationship, but the balance among the constituent elements is continuously changing. However, if there is rapid change in the strength of one or more of the elements, the equilibrium temporarily breaks down, until such time as a stable balance can be restored. This is precisely what happened in the equilibrium between students, colleges, and social policy. The relatively rapid changes in the strength of students and colleges disrupted the equilibrium. The formerly well-defined relationships among the three became muddled. At that point, the consumer philosophy was advocated as a basis for reordering the relationship and restoring the equilibrium. Current economic and demographic data indicate that these changes will continue, and in the same direction, with the result that educational consumerism will blossom in the next few years, perhaps reaching a peak in 1990, when demographic conditions will be worst for colleges and best for students. In other words, consumerism may well become the rallying cry of students for the next decade and the dominant theme governing college and university education.

5

Social Life: Individualism and the Decline of Campus Community

"Life isn't like the Brady Bunch. You get acne."
"You can't throw baseballs and footballs all your life and be happy."

In the course of this study, college students all across the country were asked what people at their school did for fun. One freshman responded by answering, "Nothing," but then quickly corrected himself with the comment "everything." Both answers made sense. "Nothing" seemed a reasonable description in view of students' rising concern with careers and grades and the fact that there is very little today's increasingly heterogeneous students do in common to have fun. "Everything" seemed correct, too. There are fewer things than ever before that this generation cannot do. The situation was masterfully, if not originally or grammatically, captured by another student, who, not overly impressed with the question, dismissed it saying, "You know, we all do our own thing."

Social Attitudes and Social Participation

This is a socially liberal generation. A majority supports expanded roles for women, legalized abortion, and the overturning of prohibitions on homosexual relations. About half favor legalization of marijuana, liberalization of divorce laws, casual (as distinguished from promiscuous) sexual relationships, and living together before marriage. In fact, this generation is more liberal about such matters than the students of the 1960s, as shown in Table 30.

It would be a mistake, though, to equate this liberalism with a richer, better, or more vibrant social life. Just the opposite appears to be true. Current student liberalism is rooted in issues of personal freedom; that is, the right of individuals to pursue their own lives without the encumbrance of external restrictions. The emphasis here is upon "me," not upon "us." The perspective tends to be a solitary one, not that of a group.

Apathy was a consistent complaint among students. It was a common complaint in the 1960s. And it has probably been a complaint as long as there have been student bodies. When groups of six to ten undergraduates at the twenty-six colleges were told that today's students have been described as apathetic and asked in what ways, if at all, this was not true at their college, seven out of every ten groups said that it was true. Most documented their assessment with stories of one or more social, civic, or political events that had failed completely.

A variety of factors draws students away from the col-

Table 30. Freshman social attitudes: 1969, 1979

	1969	*1979*
Do not believe women's activities best in the home	37	73
Favor legalized abortion	76[a]	57
Do not believe homosexual relations should be prohibited	—	54
Favor legalization of marijuana	26	50
Favor divorce liberalization	42	49
Believe sex ok if people like each other	—	49
Favor living together before marriage	—	46

[a]Since the time of the 1969 survey, abortion laws have become significantly more liberal in many parts of the country. In addition, the proabortion/right-to-life debate has politicized the issue and in this sense moved it out of the realm of social issues into the realm of political issues.
Source: ACE/UCLA Surveys, 1969, 1979.

legiate social life today. One such factor is where they live. Between 1969 and 1976, the proportion of students residing on-campus in dormitories or sorority and fraternity houses dropped by a third. During the same period, the proportion living in their own apartments or homes, excluding those residing with their parents, nearly tripled. Commuting students, those living off-campus, increased from slightly more than five out of every ten undergraduates in 1969 to nearly seven out of every ten in 1976. This is shown in Table 31. On the whole, nonresidential students tend to be far less involved in school social life. They made this clear in interviews. As one off-campus student said, "School is not the center of the universe [for me]. It is a means to an end." For many, particularly older adults, college is simply one of the obligations that have to be completed every day. Anything that is not required is not done, and social life is not required.

A second factor is work. More than half of all college students (54 percent) hold jobs, a sizeable increase (45 percent) over 1969 (Chandler, 1972, p. 81; Carnegie Surveys, 1976). In past years, when students as a group were more affluent, the time now spent on work was more often devoted to play. This point was driven home by undergraduates at Georgia State University, an urban institution whose enrollment follows the business cycle—increasing whenever the job market is poor, declining when jobs are

Table 31. Undergraduate living arrangements during the most recent college term: 1969, 1976

	1969	1976
College dormitory or other college-run housing	44%	30%[a]
Fraternity or sorority house	4	2
Rooming house or rented room	3	2
At parents' home (or other relatives)	32	28
Apartment or house (not parents)	12	34
Other	4	5

[a]U.S. Census data show that this number has declined even further ("College Students. . . ," 1979, p. 2).
Source: Carnegie Surveys, 1969, 1976.

plentiful. When asked what they did for fun, the Georgia State students' answer was an incredulous "We all work. If we wanted fun, we'd have gone to the University of Georgia."

Several related factors that discourage social life were mentioned earlier, including the rise in part-time college attendance and the increasing proportion of older undergraduates and married students, some of whom have children. As a consequence, larger portions of the student body spend less time at college, have well-developed social lives before enrolling, and shoulder other concerns outside of college which have equal or greater importance for them.

A final contributing factor is related to the campus itself. When student leaders were asked to name the major issues of concern to undergraduates today, security and parking were at the top of their lists.[1] Parking, which sounds like the punchline to a joke, is a serious and emotionally charged issue, not only for students (57 percent of whom own cars), but for faculty, too (*National On-Campus Report*, May 1978, p. 4). A case in point is a dean at one of the nation's most elite universities who spent nearly two years planning a major curriculum change. He concluded, quite seriously, that his chances of getting the new program adopted were nil, as a consequence of a recent increase in the price of faculty parking permits. The dean sounded like a man who would never again dare turn his back at a faculty meeting. Fortunately, he was wrong, and the program was adopted, at least in principle. Nonetheless, the lack of parking space and the increasing cost of gasoline together work to decrease student attendance at social events. At one urban university, institutional research found that gas and parking were among the principal factors holding down enrollment growth.

Security was another. As campuses have grown more populous, come increasingly to resemble the larger society, and become more open to their communities, crime has

---

[1]Security and parking were mentioned by 19 percent of those interviewed. Tuition and fees was named with equal frequency.

risen. At the University of Chicago and in the police district immediately surrounding it, there were 1,165 robberies, 458 assaults, and 86 rapes in 1975. At Harvard, the value of stolen property averaged between $3,000 and $4,000 a week in 1974. Of the nearly 200 serious crimes reported on the Harvard campus during one year, 128 involved robbery and assault (Lamont, 1979). The same is true at Berkeley, where crime increased dramatically in 1979, with burglaries and aggravated assaults seeing the greatest rise.

There are more student crime victims today, but there are also more student crime perpetrators. Lansing Lamont (1979, pp. 19–20) found that the annual theft rate in bookstores at several elite schools is "equal to between 3 and 4 percent of gross earnings. At Berkeley, the figure reached $150,000 a year on a $2.5 million sales volume." Harvard officials estimated that 20 to 40 percent of dormitory thefts were committed by Harvard undergraduates. Computer vandalism, destruction of personal and institutional property, and a host of other practices winked at in the past as campus pranks are costing big dollars today. An even more important consequence, though, is fear. By no stretch of the imagination can American colleges be pictured as ivory towers, particularly the urban and suburban campuses. A number of the women students interviewed complained of the danger of rape, both in terms of worry and rage. The debate over the arming of campus security guards is spreading to an ever-increasing number of colleges. Ohio State University has started a crime alert project, with 700 I.D. carrying volunteers who are trained to spot suspicious activity. To make a very long story short, crime or the fear thereof has taken a toll on student participation in extracurricular activities (*National On-Campus Report,* October 1979, p. 6). In at least one urban area, students thought the city offered a safer and richer locale for social life than their residential college.

Having Fun

All of this is not to say that campus social life is dead. Drinking ranks first when college students are asked what they do for fun, as shown in Table 32. Drinking is definitely up, and

Table 32. What college students do for fun

	Percentage of campuses at which mentioned
Drinking	77%
Dances	58
Sports/intramurals	54
Drugs	42
Parties/beach parties	38
Movies	27
Music	27
No social life/commuter school	27
Fraternities/sororities	19
Dormitory activities	19
Cards/backgammon	12
Coffee in cafeteria	12
Running	12
Concerts	12
Go to city	8
Travel/trips	8
Do your own thing	8

Note: All other sources of fun were mentioned only once.
Source: Carnegie Study, 1979.

students are starting to drink earlier. Between 1969 and 1978, the proportion of freshmen who reported drinking beer at least occasionally during the year before coming to college, a year in which the vast majority were underage, shot up from slightly more than one-half (56 percent) to nearly three-quarters (73 percent) (ACE/UCLA Surveys, 1969, 1979). Happily, though, more abusive daily drinking has remained low and fairly constant among high school seniors, at a figure of about 6 percent for the past five years (Bachman and Johnston, 1979).

Drinking among college students is another story. Particularly, though not exclusively, at residential colleges, campus group interviews reveal an almost macho ethic about consumption of alcohol, generally among men. Amid much laughter, stories of people getting stone drunk with hilarious or horrible consequences are told. At one school, students describe social life as one endless whirl of "cruisin' and boozin' "—perhaps a partial explanation for why several states have raised their legal drinking age. Hard-studying weeks and hard-drinking weekends are a common feature at a number of colleges. According to Lansing Lamont, alcohol abuse is on the rise at colleges from coast to coast. His research indicates that liquor is the number-one drug problem on campus today, arising from a combination of the need for release from academic pressures and an epidemic of despair sweeping the nation's young people. Pressure and despair—the environment could not be more supportive of alcoholism if we had planned it.

Students are much more reluctant to talk about drugs and sex. This is not particularly surprising, since both are considered more private matters, and one is illegal. Discussion about either generally has to be prodded, very gently as in pulling a tooth. And there is occasional concern that the interviewer may be a narcotics officer. Conversations about these subjects are more stilted and tense than any other. However, there are occasional revelations, like that of a dormitory called "the ski lodge" because of the liberal consumption by its occupants of cocaine, known in the vernacular as "snow."

Nonetheless, students did rank drug use, particularly marijuana, as a fairly popular way of having fun. However, drug use has changed over the past decade. It is less worshipped now, less communal, less part of a shared youth culture, and less the object of youthful rebellion. Students are less ritualistic and more matter-of-fact about drug use. They are less likely to sit in a circle passing a marijuana pipe in a dark locked room with incense and candles aglow, acid rock music blaring, and rags stuffed under the door to prevent escape of the odor. Drugs are less likely to be the sole source of an evening's entertainment. David Michaelis, a Princeton student, describes the change since the 1960s this way (1977, p. 26):

> We share few common drugs. When we go to parties, someone will always bring pot. But it is no

longer the focus of the evening. A few of us still drop acid. We are quiet about it. Speed is consumed in large quantities during exam period. Cocaine is popular, chic, and expensive ($80 a gram). We share it with one or two friends; it is never passed around. Beer and alcohol are my generation's equalizers: our Great Ice-Breakers.

Why the change? Michaelis gives one reason—"college students today have no collective identity. . . . We are out for ourselves." He believes that drugs were another generation's instrument of shared rebellion. This is certainly part of the answer, but it is an exaggeration, since the percentage of young people who have used marijuana rose substantially during the seventies.

Another part of the answer lies in earlier use of marijuana. For the generation of the 1960s, marijuana was a new experience that came later in life with much less social acceptance than it now has. Today, nearly all high school seniors have friends who have tried marijuana, six in ten have used it themselves, and one in ten use it daily or almost daily. More than one-third of all high school seniors, a constant level over the past few years, have used one or more drugs other than marijuana. Cocaine is increasingly popular—an amazing phenomenon considering its price —while use of hallucinogenics and depressants is declining (Bachman and Johnston, 1979).

A third rationale for the change comes from college students themselves. Many have heard about or witnessed drug "burnouts"—bad cases of abuse. Again, among high school seniors, three out of four strongly disapprove of experimenting with drugs harder than marijuana, most believing that such drugs pose a substantial risk to the user or others. As for marijuana, two out of three think that regular use is harmful and disapprove of it, despite the fact that such use is increasing (Bachman and Johnston, 1979, pp. 84–85). In college interviews, precisely the same sentiments are expressed.

Prudence is also the byword in sexual relationships. Sex was not included with the activities ranked on the student fun scale, but overindulgence, in the sense of promiscuity or "sleeping around," is thought to be a bad thing. When asked whether having a friend spend the night would be frowned upon, students rarely give a firm yes at nonsectarian schools, except to say that it would be unacceptable among such groups as "Bible belters" or if a woman were sleeping with many different partners. In this regard, sexism is certainly not dead. Although students at a few schools take pains to see words like "freshperson," the definition of promiscuity, with a very few notable exceptions, is defined in terms of women. Both women and men, however, speak of sexual pressure from peers to prove their liberation. They are faced with the expectation that if they are truly liberated, they must have a casual attitude about sex. One young man jokingly—but, one suspects, with an underlying seriousness—told of aggressive women picking up men and the inability to perform under such circumstances. Impotence may, indeed, be on the rise among college students. Gayness is also much more visible, as a result of graffiti, bulletin board signs, same-sex couples showing open affection, and the growth of gay groups.

Sexual activity seems much less covert today than a decade ago, with a concomitant loss of privacy. Students complain of men or women being forever in the dormitories, which makes them feel uncomfortable about wandering around in partial undress or without makeup. More extreme stories are told of students ejected from their rooms by a roommate and live-in lover or, worse yet, of students' having to live in a small room with a sexually active couple.

Dances and parties, the second and fifth most commonly mentioned fun-time pursuits, are easier for students to talk about. Music among students is big business. Each of America's 11 million college students buys an average of ten record albums a year. As to the type of music that is selling in the college market, Bruce Tannenbaun of Atlantic Records says, "Everything is selling more and more. In terms of what's become popular, rock, jazz, disco, and even classical records are selling in greater numbers than ever before. There is really no area of recorded music that is not in an upward trend. . . ." "Sales at record stores nearest to college campuses reflect the same best sellers as elsewhere in the country. However, you will see the highest percentage of total national jazz, as well as the more intelligent, esoteric, and avant-garde recordings selling at these retail stores" (Lipsius, 1979). This diversity in taste has prompted some students, like David Michaelis, to lament that his generation shares no common music, one more sign—for him and others like him—that the youth culture is vanishing (1977, p. 26).

The same could be said of popular lecturers and campus speakers. Surveys of college lecture committees and speakers bureaus "reveals a current national trend away from present global concerns . . . toward self-enhancement, self-awareness, and self-fulfillment." Celebrities and stars are popular, issues and politics are not. Comedy, inspirational topics, psychic phenomena, and the future are popular; energy, the Middle East, terrorism, and social issues are not. Feminism, journalism, poetry, and UFOs are popular; social security, illegal aliens, illiteracy, and media distortion are not. Beryl Zitch of Chicago's Contemporary Forum attributes the change to the new preoccupation with self-study, manifest in the rise of self-awareness, human potential, self-assertiveness, and self-help movements—all very popular. They are the stuff of which personal isolation derives and from which interest and openness to new ideas are stifled (Todd, 1978).

Who, then, are the top campus lecture stars of the seventies? Julian Bond, Ralph Nader, Florynce Kennedy, Jane Fonda, Dick Gregory, Bella Abzug, William Kunstler, Angela Davis, Betty Friedan, Vincent Bugliosi, Jesse Jackson, William Buckley, Caesar Chavez, and Daniel Schorr, in that order. These were named the most popular in a 1978 survey of 200 colleges and universities (*National On-Campus Report*, October 1978). The list seems to contradict all that has been said about the lecture circuit so far, since, with the exception of writer/lawyer Vincent Bugliosi, all the people on it are conspicuously political.

However, not only are they political, but they are also celebrities, newspaper and television stars, largely out of the sixties, an era with which the college students of today are preoccupied. Celebrities, not to be confused with heroes, can be brought to campus much more cheaply than name rock groups or high-priced popular comedians like Steve Martin and John Belushi. They may be political, but their present-day audience is more likely to attend their talks to see a star than to hear a message. These people are part of a concert scene that increasingly includes magic, mime, and puppet shows.

Clubs and Activities

Campus-based student clubs are still plentiful today, although they tend to be small in size. Even among the most popular of them, less than a quarter can boast a membership equal to one in twenty of their college's undergraduates. The clubs that were most popular in the 1960s tend to be among the most popular today, but over the decade there has been some shift in the themes that appeal most to students, as shown in Tables 33 and 34.

Major or career clubs and athletic, religious, and "me" groups are more popular today, while political and hobby clubs are less so. In comparison to 1969, there are more than twice as many meditation, vegetarian/macrobiotic, yoga, martial arts, and jogging clubs. Impressive gains have also been registered by hiking, skiing, crafts, local/state issue, and evangelical born-again Christian groups. Community action groups were popular in the sixties and they remain popular today. See Table 34.

At the top of the heap is intramural sports. Nearly nine out of every ten colleges have an intramural sports program, and 65 percent report an increase in student participation over the last decade. In fact, undergraduates rank intramural sports number three among the things that they do for fun.

Table 33. Popularity of different student clubs by theme: 1969, 1978

	Percentage of institutions listing one or more among the 5 most popular clubs on campus	
	1969	*1978*
Major or career groups	46%	53%
Athletic groups	26	30
Religious groups	26	28
Political groups	48	44
Me-groups (for blacks, veterans, handicapped students, international students, or other students)	51	55
Hobby/personal interest groups (crafts, music, debating, hiking, and so on)	67	60

Source: Carnegie Surveys, 1978.

Table 34. Percentage of colleges and universities with various types of clubs: 1969, 1978

	1969	*1978*
Intramural sports	83%	88%
Performing arts groups	68	73
Preprofessional clubs	63	67
Community action groups	43	48
Evangelical born-again Christian groups	20	38
Ski clubs	32	43
Hiking/outdoor clubs	25	38
Meditation groups	13	26
Crafts groups	15	22
Jogging clubs	6	21
Yoga groups	8	18
International issues groups	23	18
Local or state issues groups	12	17
National issues groups	21	17
Vegetarian/macrobiotic groups	4	10
Antiwar/peace groups	31	6

Source: Carnegie Surveys, 1978.

At Berkeley, a school whose reputation does not rest entirely upon its athletic prowess, participation in intramural sports is increasing even faster than business school enrollments. In 1969–70, the program, in which participation rates had previously averaged in the low twenty-thousand-hour range, dropped to 10–12,000 hours, much of the schedule being cancelled due to the massive antiwar strikes. In 1979, participation in the program was again limited, this time by lack of space and the 101,000-hour participation rate, a nearly fourfold increase over 1970–71. A ceiling was placed on the program, and waiting lists are currently so long that new facilities are on the drawing board, although one does not hear much talk about building from sane people in higher education at the present time. In fact, it is not unusual to see a line of 100 to 150 people at 7:30 a.m. waiting about 45 minutes to register for an hour's use of a racquetball court the next day.

Racquetball is the fastest-growing new sport on the Berkeley campus, but there are also now ten different martial arts groups, frisbee, yoga, and much, much more, in addition to softball, football, and other familiar games. Coeducational teams are booming. Women's teams are not. The desire for all women's recreational sports has not increased, despite campus feminism. The increased classroom competition was already being reflected on the playing field a few years ago. To ease the problem, a noncompetitive recreational intramural league was created. However, it was not an overwhelming success—only about one in every ten students chose to participate.

The growth in intramural sports at Berkeley, one consequence of this generation's interest in health, physical fitness, and self-improvement, is being mirrored across the country. In the past few years, membership in the National Intramural Recreational Sports Association has quintupled.

Fraternities and sororities are also growing. To anyone who has watched television in recent years or seen the movie *Animal House,* they may seem the centerpiece of collegiate social life, but this is not the case. Fraternities and sororities are by no means omnipresent on college campuses. Fewer than four in ten colleges (37 percent) have them (Carnegie Surveys, 1978). In fact, this country's very visible national fraternities, whose current members and living alumni total three million, are found on only 604 campuses. However, their chapters are multiplying, as they have for decades (see Table 35).

Despite this expansion of the number of chapters, the late 1960s were a bad time for fraternity membership. Student participation actually fell between 1965 and 1971. In 1965, average chapter size was 49 members, but by 1971, when the decline hit bottom, membership reached a low of 34 per chapter. It has taken until today to return to the mid-1960s level. Accordingly, what now looks like a dramatic rise in fraternity interest and participation actually represents nothing more than the reemergence of the status quo. Finally, relative to the total college population, fraternity membership is significantly smaller today than it was in 1965.

It is impossible to speak as concretely about campus religious groups. Participation rates are unknown, but the groups themselves are mushrooming. They come in a variety of stripes—counterculture groups such as yoga and transcendental meditation; personal growth groups like est (Erhardt Seminars Training) and primal screaming; and neo-Christian groups such as Jews for Jesus and Campus Crusade for Christ (Wuthnow, 1976). Between 1969 and 1978, Berkeley added at least twelve new religious groups to

**Table 35. Number of national fraternity
chapters in the United States**

Year	Number of chapters
1941	2,445
1951	3,055
1965	3,838
1974	4,341
1979	4,800

Source: Unpublished data, National Interfraternity Council.

its list of institutionally registered clubs. The accent was distinctly Christian and included a range of organizations such
as the Chinese Christian Fellowship, Just Christians, The
Way, Divine Light Experience, Collegiates for Christ, and the
Radical Jewish Union. By 1969, Berkeley already had representatives of most of the counterculture groups mentioned,
while participation in personal growth groups appears to rest
more on individual initiative and to occur more frequently
off-campus. Signs advertising religious meetings and religious clubs are a more common feature today on campus
bulletin boards at all types of colleges than they were a few
years ago. And while not observed on campus at any institution visited, such cults as the Society for Krishna Consciousness and Reverend Sun Myung Moon's Unification Church,
were found to be operating at the border of several.

Nevertheless, religious commitment among college students seems to be dropping. Although the majority of
freshmen (58 percent) believe that the nation's churches are
doing a good job, some freshmen feel that organized religion
is responsible for considerable dishonesty/immorality (18
percent) and that it should have less influence (12 percent)
(Bachman and Johnston, 1979, p. 86). Attendance at religious services is down slightly in comparison to the late
1960s. Eighty-four percent of freshmen went to services at
least occasionally in 1978 versus 89 percent in 1969 (ACE/
UCLA Surveys; 1969, 1979). Even more to the point, students in the 1970s are twice as likely to say that they are opposed or indifferent to religion (30 percent) as that they are
deeply committed (15 percent). At the same time, the proportion of college students who state no religious prefer-
ences has risen noticeably (15 percent in 1969 versus 21 percent in 1976) (Carnegie Surveys; 1969, 1976).

This leads to a seeming paradox—religions proliferate,
yet student interest in religion declines. However, it is not
much of a paradox. When faith or interest in traditional religion declines, new religions are a common
development, particulary when trust in normally competing
social institutions is low. To a subgroup of young people look-

ing for something to believe in, nontraditional religions with an emphasis on community or a well-defined dogma for guidance have been particularly appealing. In 1976, one in every twenty college students belonged to a nontraditional religious group outside the Protestant, Catholic, or Jewish faiths. The rise of neo-Christian groups, which owes much to the post–Vietnam/Watergate malaise, is a similar phenomenon, involving the rejuvenation of an existing religion rather than its wholesale rejection. Today nearly one in three college freshmen describes himself or herself as a reborn Christian (ACE/UCLA Survey, 1979).

Others attribute the religious revival at least in part to a reaction against drugs, liquor, and sex. In this sense, the religious revival is an instrument for avoiding the excesses of others, a safe harbor after a bad experience, or legitimation, conscious or unconscious, for abstinence in a peer culture that views such behavior as antisocial.

On the basis of these data, one could certainly conclude that college social life resembles social life of the 1960s more than it differs. Then, as now, students drank coffee, listened to records, dated, danced, went to films and concerts, and walked romantically about the campus arm in arm. Sex, drugs, religion, sports, fraternities, and sororities were part of the campus scene in the sixties and continue to be so today. Popular movies and old favorites like *Casablanca, Citizen Kane,* W. C. Fields, Charlie Chaplin, and the Marx Brothers were in vogue in both periods. All of the things that college students did to have fun a decade ago, they do for fun today. Nonetheless, new activities—like jogging, practiced by every student interviewed at the University of Oregon—have become fashionable, and old ones—such as streaking—have become passé. In colleges and universities, as in a kaleidoscope, the pieces remain the same, but their configuration is always changing. What stands out in today's configuration is diversity, individualism, escapism, and searching. Although these qualities were present 10 years ago, they are more distinctly visible now.

Diversity is apparent both in the plethora of activities

that students enjoy and in the conditions which preclude some of them from pursuing a campus social life. Students are more different now as individuals than they were before. They have little sense of a shared collegiate culture. They are a group for which both drinking and praying are growth industries. As a group, they have very liberal attitudes about personal freedoms. Even in the group activities they pursue, "me" stands out. With sex the most intimate of group activities, there is the selfish theft of the privacy of others such as roommates, increasing demands by participants for self-fulfillment, and complaints of aggressive manipulation of partners in pursuit of personal liberation. Increased competition in the classroom is paralleled by increased competition on the playing field. Escapism and searching are inseparably intertwined. One person's escape is another's haven at the end of a long search. Health and religious movements confirm their indivisibility.

This stands out in the foreground of today's kaleidoscope, although it may only be what strikes the eye after a long look at the configuration of the 1960s, or it may only be what stands out as foreign or different. In the background, there are ever so many conflicting images: popular community action groups, successful blood drives, interest in charitable causes, and enormous enthusiasm for Big Brother and Big Sister programs. These too are plainly discernible, but they recede into the background when one views the whole. An indisputable, even an important part of today's campus social motif, they are by no means its dominant theme.

Perhaps nothing illustrates this thesis more than the changing content of campus bookstores. These stores are a treasure trove of information about academic programming and the demands and expectations that faculty have of their students. More germane to this chapter, they are also exhibition halls of student tastes, where the latest fads replace the popular wares of yesterday, which disappear as quickly and as quietly as last week's newspaper.

In the past decade, there have been a number of visible changes. The first may be noticeable right at the door, where there is an electronic or even a human security system designed to reduce theft. In some stores there are entirely new departments—athletic counters chock-full of expensive jogging shoes, tennis rackets, skateboards, roller skates, and sporting accessories; counters where calculators, ranging from the miniprice to the maxiservice, replace the late slide rule; and T-shirt salons where garments advertising all kinds of commercial products—beer, trucks, rock stars, and restaurants—are the rage.

Eventually one arrives at that part of the store where books are actually sold, which tends to be the dominant feature at most schools. Along with the traditional subject-matter signs that one normally sees—"fiction," "political science," "mystery"—there is a whole host of new ones, including "women," "mysticism," "lifestyles," "environment and energy," "health," "people," and "self-help." Some of the more familiar subject-matter areas have increased their shelf space or even earned signs of their own. Among these are film/media, science fiction, religion, China, sports/exercise, dieting, and Marxism. New magazines have appeared in the periodical racks—*People, Self, Ms., Runners World, Playgirl, Penthouse,* and *High Times.* Radical critiques of American society like those of a decade ago by Abbie Hoffman, Jerry Rubin, and Eldridge Cleaver are less prominent, and one sees fewer political titles in general.

The patrons look different, too. On the whole they are much better dressed. As one student, Christy Hoppe of the University of Texas, noted, "The patched jeans or tattered shirts which were apparently held together by memories, if not much else, are scarcely visible now. They've been replaced by fashionable rugby shirts and prefaded jeans" (Michaelis, 1977).

These changes are a sign of the times. They have not all occurred at every bookstore, but only a very few stores have managed to avoid them entirely. The birth of new interests and the death of old concerns is a reflection of the changing world of the college student. The increased emphasis on the individual, which is evident in magazines like *Self* and the many self-help books, is an accurate reflection of the turning inward of students. The growing volume of escapist literature—science fiction, fantasy, drug and celebrity magazines, film, and the like—satisfies a deep hunger on college and university campuses across the country. One senses that many students are searching, in some cases rather desperately, for something to hold on to, something to believe in. This is mirrored in the rash of books on mysticism, Marx, religion, exercise, sex, health, women, and self-help. These volumes provide answers rather than raising additional questions—appropriate to a time when people are yearning for simple truths.

6

The Future: Going First Class on the Titanic

Interviewer: Will the United States be a better or worse place to live in the next ten years?
Student: The U.S. will definitely be a worse place to live.
Interviewer: Then you must be pessimistic about the future.
Student: No, I'm optimistic.
Interviewer (with surprise): Why?
Student: Because I have a high grade point average and I'm going to get a good job, make a lot of money, and live in a nice house.

This conversation was repeated on campuses all across the country. Put simply, college students are optimistic about their personal futures but pessimistic about the future of the country. This is the conclusion of several recent studies. In campus group interviews, 91 percent of the students say they are optimistic about themselves, but only 41 percent are optimistic about the country. All the rest are either pessimistic or mixed (Carnegie Study, 1979). Freshmen surveys confirm this as well. For the past four years, the Institute for Social Research at the University of Michigan has studied the future outlook of college-bound high school seniors. With each succeeding year, students have grown slightly more pessimistic about the country, until 1979, when pessimism increased by a full fifth. In contrast, as in the campus interviews, nine out of every ten students were quite positive about their own futures (Bachman and Johnston, 1979).

When asked what they were apprehensive about, undergraduates listed everything under the sun—and that, too, if one counts solar energy. They were fearful of the economy, pollution, energy, crime, morals, and nuclear war. They were concerned about nuclear power, corporations, greed, illegal aliens, and the right wing. Anita Bryant and her antihomosexual campaign, Phyllis Schlafly and her anti-equal-rights-amendment campaign, and California and its antitax Proposition 13 were mentioned; so were waste, the poor, foreign policy, self-centeredness, divorce, money, authoritarianism, and prices. Students were worried about drugs, increased regulation, permissiveness, reduced standards of living, the environment, and the justice system—these and much, much more were on their list.

The prevalent mood of despair is captured in a story told by a college senior who fell asleep one night while watching television. He awoke with a start some time later to the sound of an emergency warning signal blaring from the television set. It was, to be sure, a test, but the student did not know this, having slept through the announcement. His reaction was one of sheer terror. Seconds later, on hearing that it was "only a test," he became embarrassed at his overreaction. Then he grew frightened once again, this time because the warning could easily have been legitimate: it could have signaled a war, a nuclear plant accident, a terrorist attack, a toxic chemical spill, or any of a dozen other catastrophes. He was frightened in the second instance because there was no good reason to believe that next time the signal would be only a test.

There is a sense among today's undergraduates that they are passengers on a sinking ship, a Titanic if you will, called the United States or the world. Perhaps this is part of the reason why suicide has become the second leading cause of death among students in the 1970s, exceeded only by accidents. Be that as it may, today's fatalism fuels a spirit of justified hedonism. There is a growing belief among college students that, if they are doomed to ride on the Titanic, they ought at least to make the trip as pleasant—make that as lavish—as possible and go first class, for they assume there is nothing better.

Concern for Money

Going first class is expensive. Today's college students know this and are more interested in earning money than their predecessors; so say a majority of freshmen. This past decade witnessed a one-third increase in the proportion of first-year students for whom being well off financially is an essential or very important objective. In 1969, 45 percent of freshmen expressed this opinion. By 1979, 63 percent did (ACE/UCLA Surveys, 1969, 1979). Among all undergraduates, two out of three say that being well-off financially is important to them (Carnegie Surveys, 1976).

For this generation, going first class means consumer goods aplenty. Between seven and eight out of every ten college freshmen say that having the latest fashions, records, sporting goods, and books is very or pretty important to them. This is by no means the result of past deprivation, for this is not a generation which has lacked for material goods. A majority of freshmen earned $100 a month or more in their senior year of high school. This was largely discretionary money. Students enjoy having money and they enjoy spending it. In fact, among college freshmen, three-quarters of the women and about half as many of the men describe themselves as very fond of shopping for clothes, records, and other popular items. The others confess to liking such activities only slightly less; that is, pretty much (Bachman and Johnston, 1979).

College students make up more than 5 percent of the total United States population and more than 7 percent of the population aged 17 and over. This is no secret to the advertising and marketing community. An analysis of student newspapers at twenty-six colleges and universities reveals the

wide variety of advertisements aimed at the college market.
As Table 36 indicates, most prominent are ads for local shops
and events, which comprise more than three out of five of
the commercial appeals. However, beer and liquor advertisements are the most conspicuous, for usually they take up
a full page and occasionally they include a colorful poster-
sized insert just right for hanging in a student's room. Also
represented are such services as typing, training in speed-

**Table 36. Content of advertisements in 26 college and
university student newspapers: 1979[a]**

	Percentage of total advertisements
Local shops	52%
Local events	8
Services (for example, typing and speedreading)	5
Jobs	5
Movies	5
Travel	4
Beer and liquor	4
Abortion and legal services	4
Charity solicitations	3
Armed forces	3
Preparatory courses (for example, preparation for graduate and professional school tests)	2
Peace Corps or Vista	2
Banks	1
Religion	1
Blood drives	1
Cars	<1
Camps	<1
Books/magazines	<1
Research volunteer needs/research services (term paper writing)	<1
Radio stations	<1
Credit cards	<1

[a]Based on 1,213 advertisements.
Source: Carnegie Study, 1979.

reading, jobs, movies, travel, abortion and legal counseling, the military, banks, cars, charities, religion, and credit cards (Carnegie Study, 1979).

The importance of the student market is well illustrated by a recent occurrence at Stanford University. The student government was asked to boycott Coors beer at all on-campus events owing to allegations of bad labor practices. When word reached the local distributor, he arranged for five students to go on a fact-finding tour of the plant in Colorado, nearly a thousand miles away, at Coors' expense (*National On-Campus Report,* March 1979, p. 3).

As to what can be expected of these students after college, the Institute for Social Research at the University of Michigan concludes more of the same (Bachman and Johnston, 1979, p. 82):

> "A majority appear committed to the 'American Dream.' They want their own home (not an apartment or a condominium) with a big yard, well-kept lawn, appliances, stereo, and the like. About half think it is extremely important to have clothes in the latest style. And nearly all want to own a car—though not necessarily a large or a late model one.

Educational and Career Goals

This growing concern with the material joys of life is not reflected in increasing educational aspirations. The belief that "the more you learn, the more you earn" is perhaps a relic of an earlier day. Table 37 shows that student educational plans are much the same as they were in the late 1960s. There is a notable rise, however, in the proportion of students seeking professional degrees in medicine and law. Also of interest are the very real changes in aspirations among women. In every category of doctoral degree, more women now want them than in 1969. The growth is largest for law degrees, where the increase has been ninefold, and for medical degrees, which are more than three times as popular. This is shown in

Table 37. Freshman educational aspirations—highest degree planned:
1969, 1979

	Percent of freshmen choosing	
	1969	1979
None	2%	2%
Associate	9	7
Bachelor's	38	37
Master's	33	32
Ph.D., Ed.D.	10	9
M.D., D.O., D.D.S., D.V.M.	4	6
LL.B., J.D.	1	4
B.D., M.Div.	<1	<1
Other	2	2

Source: ACE/UCLA Surveys, 1969, 1979.

Table 38. Educational aspiration is an obvious area where
the women's liberation/equality movement has been quite
potent.

Another area is careers. In the late 1960s, teaching was
by far the top job choice among women students. Almost
four out of ten (37 percent) freshmen women said it would
be their probable future occupation. Today, teaching still
ranks number one, but only for one in every ten female
freshmen. As a matter of fact, being a business executive (8
percent) or a nurse (7 percent) are more popular careers for
women than elementary (7 percent) or secondary school
teaching (3 percent). This was not even remotely the case ten
years ago (ACE/UCLA Surveys; 1969, 1979).

However, it would be a mistake to equate plans with reality. It seems likely that fewer students in the 1960s and
more students in the 1970s did in fact enter teaching than
indicated by their plans. In the 1960s, encouragement for the
choice of teaching as a career came both from fellow students
and from parents. Today, economic and demographic conditions have changed the minds of many parents, and expand-
ing women's consciousness and a shrinking market for
teachers have changed the campus mood. The result is that
fewer students in the 1960s actually reached the state of de-

Table 38. Female freshman educational aspirations—highest degree planned: 1969, 1979

	Percent choosing	
	1969	*1979*
None	2%	2%
Associate	11	9
Bachelor's	44	38
Master's	33	32
Ph.D., Ed.D.	6	8
M.D., D.O., D.D.S., D.V.M.	2	6
LL.B., J.D.	<1	4
B.D., M.Div.	<1	<1
Other	2	2

Source: ACE/UCLA Surveys, 1969, 1979.

sired grace—becoming a teacher—and that more students in the 1970s are choosing to buck the tide.

Women are bucking another tide, too: the tide of <u>sex stereotyping in the job market</u>. Increasing numbers are planning on jobs in business, law, medicine, and other professions, which traditionally were men's jobs. There has been a rapid and dramatic decline in the percentage of college students, male and female, who plan on being full-time "housewives." Between 1969 and 1976, the proportion choosing this line of work fell from 8 percent to 2 percent (Carnegie Surveys, 1969, 1976).

The magic word in career choice today is "professional." Relative to the late 1960s, accounting, business, law, optometry, pharmacy, and most other professions which are not in the nether world of the job market are growing. This is shown in Table 39. According to the Institute for Social Research, two out of three freshmen in 1979 are planning on careers in the professions, and one out of five hopes to enter one of the platinum professions—law or medicine.

If the philosophy guiding this generation is not "The more you learn, the more you earn," it is certainly something on the order of "<u>Learn the right thing and earn a lot of money</u>." A college sophomore echoed the opinion of a

Table 39. Student career plans in selected fields: 1969, 1976

	Percent choosing	
	1969	*1976*
Physician, surgeon, dentist	3%	4%
Lawyer	3	4
Social welfare	2	3
Teacher	17	12
Business executive	7	10
Engineer	5	5
Pharmacist/optician	<1	1
Accountant	2	5
Homemaker	8	2

Source: Carnegie Surveys, 1969, 1976.

number of the students interviewed, though by no means a majority, when she said, "Sure, I want an interesting job, but money is the key. Money is nice. Poor is not nice."

In the course of this study, faculty at several of the highest-ranking graduate departments in the country complained bitterly that quality students are just not applying to their departments. The quality students are being shanghaied by the professional schools. Harvard sociologist David Riesman has described this phenomenon as America's brain drain. The cream of America's young people, the most exciting and intellectually curious college students, are now choosing professional school over graduate school because of the superior rewards and brighter employment prospects. At an engineering school, for example, a group of seven upperclassmen spoke with us about their job plans. Six were interested in engineering or technical management careers, which would involve teaming their undergraduate engineering degree with a master's in business administration. The seventh thought he might like to get a Ph.D. in engineering and then teach at the university level. The others expressed surprise and tried to talk him out of it. One explained to him that his decision was economically wrong: A Ph.D. would take longer to earn than an M.B.A. and be worth much less—even less than a bachelor's degree in engineering alone. Others said that such a move would be "weird" and tried to apply a little peer pressure. Still others tried ridicule, lambasting him for refusing to leave the university cocoon and enter the real world of business. At least ten minutes were spent in trying to change his mind. The discussion was lighthearted, but the conflict was real. In the end, the student said that he was uncertain. The fact of the matter was that most of the group could not comprehend why anyone would choose to teach rather than manage. More than that, they were offended by the irrationality of their peer's choice.

Aside from the money, part of the allure of management and the professions is the glitter. An anticipated fringe benefit of traveling first class, this translates into a status profession, personal recognition, professional acclaim, and an opportunity to make decisions and manage a staff. The desire by students for work-related accomplishments and honest-to-goodness achievements seems pale in comparison to the wish to attain the enumerated outcomes usually associated with them, which have increased since the 1960s. By a factor of never less than three and sometimes as much as six, as Table 40 shows, students would rather become authorities in their field or obtain recognition from their colleagues than make a theoretical contribution to science, create artistic works, achieve in the performing arts, or write original works.

Social Values and Family Plans

Glitter and gold are part of the driving force for this generation, more so than for their predecessors of the 1960s, but nobler motivations and a more altruistic spirit are present as well. Nearly two out of three freshmen think that it is essential or very important to help others who are in trouble. There has been only a slight decline in this regard since 1969 (ACE/UCLA Surveys, 1969, 1979). That lack of change, along with the more visible me-orientation of the present, has tended to minimize, and even to mask, the more selfless inclinations among college students today. These inclinations

Table 40. Freshman life objectives: 1969, 1979

| | Percent describing objective as essential or very important | |
	1969	1979
Be an authority in my field	59%	73%
Help others in difficulty	66	64
Raise a family	71	65
Develop a philosophy of life	82	53
Obtain recognition from my colleagues	41	52
Be successful in my own business	46	49
Have administrative responsibility	24	37
Influence social values	34	32
Influence political structure	16	15
Make theoretical contribution to science	10	14
Create artistic works	16	14
Achieve in a performing art	11	12
Write original works	16	12

Source: ACE/UCLA Surveys, 1969, 1979.

are real and they are likely to continue. The degree to which they will be translated into action is another story. The shift in opinion regarding assistance to minorities and aid to crime victims that was discussed earlier, makes one wonder what will happen when this generation faces a head-to-head confrontation between the glitter and gold and succor for the needy.

The signs auger badly, but they are by no means clear. The nonmaterial is less important to current students than their counterparts of the 1960s. Freshmen now are much less interested in developing a philosophy of life, as shown in Table 40. In 1969, 82 percent of first year students thought that this was very important or essential. Today 53 percent do. That is still a majority, but the decline amounts to a hefty 29 percent (ACE/UCLA Surveys, 1969, 1979). Perhaps if one believes that he or she is trapped on a doomed ship, a philosophy of life becomes meaningless—not so different from the old cliche of rearranging the chairs on the deck of the

Titanic. It is a world where freedom of individual action seems pathetically limited and a time when situational ethics appear to make more sense than a philosophy of life. For nearly all college students (87 percent), life has dimensions that simply cannot be grasped rationally. To this Doonesbury offers the advice, "Go with the flow" (Carnegie Surveys, 1976). A philosophy of life does not seem to be particularly necessary or even very helpful in such a world.

The fact of the matter is that almost half of all college students feel helpless to control the world in which they live. Forty-nine percent agree that an individual can do little to bring about change in our society (Carnegie Surveys, 1976). Again, as shown in Table 40, slightly fewer first-year students now than a decade ago consider it important to influence social values or political structure. Only one out of three students would influence social values and one out of seven cares to grapple with political structures (ACE/UCLA Surveys: 1969, 1979).

In these and in many other ways, undergraduates express a sense of being alone, which should not be confused with a sense of being lonely. Only three out of ten would describe themselves as lonely, and that represents a slight decrease over 1969 (Carnegie Surveys, 1969, 1976). There is a curious ambivalence here. Students both complain about and glorify the "captain of my soul" ethic. That is, they are proud of being able to withstand the bludgeoning of chance and fate, but at the same time they are sad that they have to do so. Attitudes about marriage and child rearing are a good reflection of this. For no more than a handful of the women participating in the campus interviews is marriage their prime goal after college. In fact, nationally, 97 percent of all students say they plan to have a career after school (Carnegie Surveys, 1976). There has been a sharp drop in the proportion of college freshmen who say they plan to get married while in college (6 percent) or within a year of leaving college (18 percent) (ACE/UCLA Surveys, 1969, 1979). As shown in Table 41, this is true for men as well as women.

A combination of factors explains this. Part of the

Table 41. Freshman attitudes about marriage and family: 1969, 1979

| | *Percent agreeing* | | | | | |
| | *Total* | | *Men* | | *Women* | |
	1969	*1979*	*1969*	*1979*	*1969*	*1979*
Plan to marry while in college	7%	5%	10%	4%	8%	6%
Plan to marry within a year of college	18	16	24	13	21	18
Raising a family is very important or essential to me	67	65	78	65	71	65

Source: ACE/UCLA Surveys, 1969, 1979.

rationale is the women's movement, which has brought new confidence to many women and made them much more eager to pursue opportunities outside of the home and even outside of marriage. Men have, no doubt, learned similar lessons from it as well. Then, too, there are the pressures to survive or to earn glitter and gold in an environment perceived as hostile. As one college senior said, "I can't take care of me. How am I going to take care of someone else?" Decreased interest in marriage is caused in part by a change in attitudes—a healthy independence associated with the women's movement and similar causes; in part by fear of encumbering additional responsibilities—added weight that might decrease one's chances of swimming to safety at a later date; and in part by bravado—like the cowboy who can kiss all the girls but must, according to Western convention, ride off in the sunset alone with his horse, which in this day and age is replaced by a car. And it is also peer pressure. An anecdote was told on a couple of campuses about a woman student who burst into tears before an administrator or teacher, saying that she wanted very much to get married but that she could not mention it to her dormmates because their opinions would be so negative. She could not even tell her boyfriend, the intended. Her real concern was not having to hide her feelings but rather the fear that having such feelings was unnatural or sick. The most negative attitudes toward marriage are encountered at selective schools where students have the highest career aspirations and women's politics are most strongly rooted, but this very negative reaction toward marriage is not the situation at all colleges. At one southern college, a freshman made it clear that she came to school to find a husband. If she did not make substantial progress toward this goal during the first year, she would leave because of the high tuition and fees.

Opinions about childrearing are similar, but the sentiments are sharper. Among college freshmen, nearly seven out of ten say that raising a family is very important or essential to them. This represents only a slight decline over the past decade (ACE/UCLA Surveys, 1969, 1979). Having children came up infrequently and always in the same way during our group interviews. When asked about future plans, women would occasionally say, much in the way of an afterthought, that they certainly did not want children. What was startling was the anger and vehemence of these women, most of whom seemed quite apolitical. Behind their statements was the potential of being victimized—victimized by men who would not share even half the responsibility for raising children, victimized by a society so evil as to make it undesirable to bring children into the world, and victimized by the children themselves who would halt their mother's careers and put a serious crimp in their social lives.

These few women were not the only students who talked about becoming victims. They merely spoke about it louder and more directly. Being a victim was a theme in student discussions of politics, particularly of the lessons learned from Vietnam and Watergate and of the rationale for me-groups. It was an element in students' conversation about education, especially of career pressures and competition for grades. And it was an aspect of their considerations about the future, the stuff upon which the Titanic mentality rests. Perhaps David Michaelis was wrong when he said that beer was his generation's great equalizer. The great equalizer may instead be fear of becoming one of the victims.

7

Conclusions: A Retrospective, A Prospective, and A Recommendation

---

My generation is disillusioned. . . . The acceleration of life for us has been so great that into the last few years have been crowded the experiences and the ideas of a normal lifetime. We have in our unregenerate youth learned the practicality and the cynicism that is safe only in unregenerate old age. We have been forced to become realists overnight, instead of idealists, as was our birthright. We have seen man at his lowest. . . . We have been forced to question, and in many cases to discard, the religion of our fathers. We have seen hideous peculation, greed, anger, hatred, malice, and all uncharitableness, unmasked and rampant and unashamed. We have been forced to live in an atmosphere of "tomorrow we die," and so, naturally, we drank and were merry. We have seen the rottenness and shortcomings of old governments. . . . In short, we have seen the inherent beastliness of the human race revealed in an infernal apocalypse.

—F. Scott Fitzgerald, 1920

• In 1920, writing about the postwar generation, F. Scott Fitzgerald described them as "grown up to find all gods dead, all wars fought, all faith in men shaken. . . . Young students try to believe in older authors, constituents try to believe in their Congressmen, countries try to believe in their statesmen, but they can't." Here was a new generation . . . grown up to find all gods dead, all wars fought, all faiths in men shaken. (On the post-World War I generation by F. Scott Fitzgerald, 1920, p. 282, 215.)

• "The mood of the country was hedonistic," William Leuchtenburg has noted. "Omar Khayyam's quatrains took the colleges by storm. . . . Youth . . . tried to escape the inexorability of time. One of the younger generation, replying to its critics, observed: 'The trouble with them is that they can't seem to realize that we are busy, that what pleasure we snatch must be incidental and feverishly hurried. We have to make the most of our time. . . . We must gather rosebuds while we may'" (1958, p. 174).

• In 1935, the Carnegie Foundation for the Advancement of Teaching observed, "The student on campus . . . is a hardworking, serious-minded person who demands more of the college library, the laboratory, and the instructor than did his brother of a decade ago" (p. 6). And one year later, the editors of *Fortune* lamented, "The present-day college generation is fatalistic . . . will not stick its neck out. . . . If we take the mean average to be the truth, it is a cautious, subdued, unadventurous generation, unwilling to storm heaven, afraid to make a fool of itself, unable to dramatize its predicament. . . . Security is the summum bonum of the present college generation" ("The College Student," 1936, p. 100).

Today's college students, taken in aggregate like those of the twenties and thirties, resemble every other college generation in some respects and are unlike any other in other ways. A few of its characteristics have persisted since the days of America's first college students. Others have oscillated, changing periodically throughout nearly 350 years of collegiate history. And some of this generation's characteristics are unique.

Commonalities

As in prerevolutionary times, the dominant campus group, culturally if no longer numerically, remains white males of upper- and middle-class background—a pattern broken only during major wars. Some nontraditional students have always sought higher education—in the days of the colonial colleges, they were the children of artisans, seamen, slaves, and small farmers—and they continue to do so. Parents still occasionally send their unruly children away to school in the hopes of improving discipline or developing a bit of sophistication, and they are probably as often disappointed as their colonial ancestors. Students' reasons for attending college have not changed much, even if the preference for certain colleges and the character of the colleges themselves have. Student activism, once euphemistically called rowdiness, existed in the earliest colleges and continues to the present. Then as now, however, activists comprised only a minority of undergraduates. The extracurricular life of students continues as it always has to supplement the academic life of the college. When institutions were intellectually weaker than students would have liked, the extracurriculum stressed the intellectual. When colleges deemphasized the religious or social or physical, the extracurriculum became its home. This is still the case. Fraternities, which date back to the eighteenth century, are alive and well today, and residential college life remains vibrant, though a bit the worse for wear. In these ways, today's generation is precisely like all the students who have come before.

Oscillations

Societies are like people. They go through periods of wakeful, strenuous, and even frenetic activity, and then must rest. A period of waking, a period of rest, a period of waking, a period of rest—the cycle goes on and on. In this century, war has been the dividing line, marking the end of wakefulness —a final outpouring of frenzied activity—and the beginning of rest—the onset of exhausted slumber.

Periods of waking are change oriented and reform

minded. More than this, they are what were described in Chapter Two as times of community ascendancy. Recall that such periods tend to be more future oriented and ascetic. They emphasize duty to others, responsibility, and the propriety of giving. In this century, there have been three such periods—the progressive era from around 1904 through World War I, the Roosevelt/depression years from 1932 through World War II, and "the 1960s" from about 1957 into the Vietnam War. These periods were known in their own time by such names as the Square Deal, the New Freedom, the New Deal, the New Frontier, and the Great Society. Such periods tend to be times offering a sense of movement, excitement, adventure, and perhaps even magic. Their theme is promise, and their leaders are charismatic.

Periods of rest have occurred after World War I, after World War II, and after the Vietnam War. These are times in which people are tired, having been asked for years to give, and give more, and finally, if necessary, to give lives—their own, their families', or their friends'—to fight a war. People are weary and want a break. Thoughts and actions that were directed outward turn inward to concerns that have been neglected—to getting one's life or the life of one's family in order. These are times that in Chapter Two were called periods of individual ascendancy. They tend to be more present oriented, more hedonistic than ascetic, more concerned with rights than with responsibilities, more interested in duty to one's self than to others, and more dedicated to the propriety of taking rather than giving. In such eras national government tends to be less colorful. With the exception of the Harding administration, which promised a "return to normalcy," these periods have been known by a president's name, not by a slogan or motto. Such times tend to be pragmatic. They promise personal freedom, and their leaders are usually managers who can solve problems themselves while giving the public a chance to rest. (See Figure 2.)

Colleges, like all other social institutions, and students, like the rest of the population, follow these cycles. General student character varies from periods of community as-

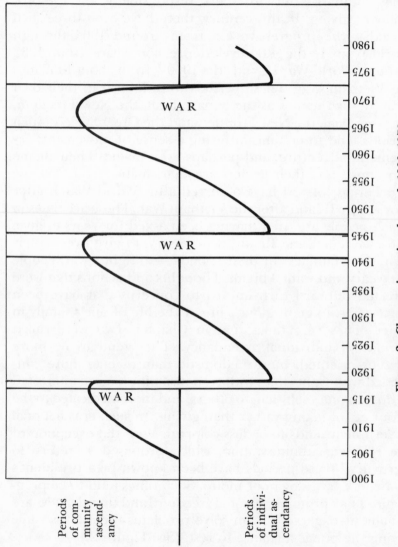

Figure 2. Changes in national mood: 1900–1979

cendancy to periods of individual acendancy, and today's students exhibit the characteristics typical of individual acendancy:

- During periods of individual ascendancy, students are less activist than in periods of community ascendancy, as shown in Figure 3, which plots Philip Altbach's calculation of the extent of student activism from 1900 to 1970, based on his numerous studies of the period.
- During periods of individual ascendancy, student politics are more centrist or middle-of-the-road. Ideological and political interest is relatively low. The proportion of undergraduates who are politically far right, far left, or adherents of idologies of any type decreases. Isolationism grows and international concern declines during such times.
- During periods of individual ascendancy, students are more socially oriented than serious. Membership in fraternities and sororities rises. Sports and intercollegiate athletics grow in popularity. Drinking increases. Fads are more likely to occur—flagpole sitting, Mah-Jongg, and marathon dance contests in the 1920s; pantyraids, piano wrecking, and telephone booth stuffing during the 1950s; and streaking, skateboarding, and toga parties in the 1970s.
- During periods of individual ascendancy, student social attitudes tend to be more liberal, allowing for increased personal freedom. The 1920s were the age of women smoking, increased sexual freedom, and Freud. The 1940s and 1950s, aside from inaugurating the pill and pantyraids, were a time when students, particularly returning veterans, fought strenuously against hazing and rules based on the in loco parentis doctrine. The 1970s were a period in which concern with freedom was perhaps the hallmark of the era, as discussed in Chapters Two and Five.
- During periods of individual ascendancy, students are more likely to be involved in religious activities, and campuses are more prone to experience religious revivals and to serve as launching pads for new religious movements. This is pointed out in Figure 4.

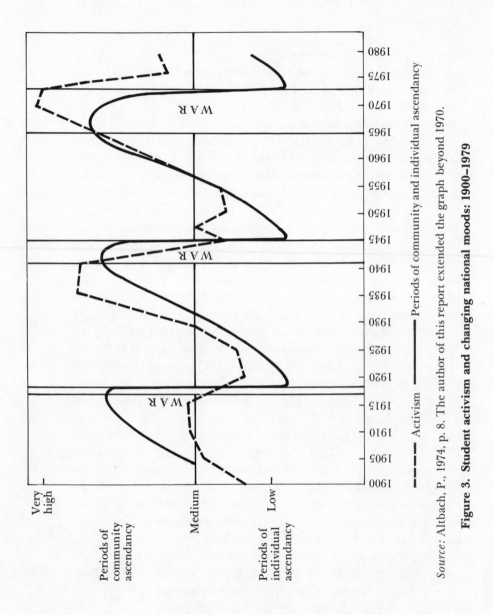

Source: Altbach, P., 1974, p. 8. The author of this report extended the graph beyond 1970.

Figure 3. Student activism and changing national moods: 1900–1979

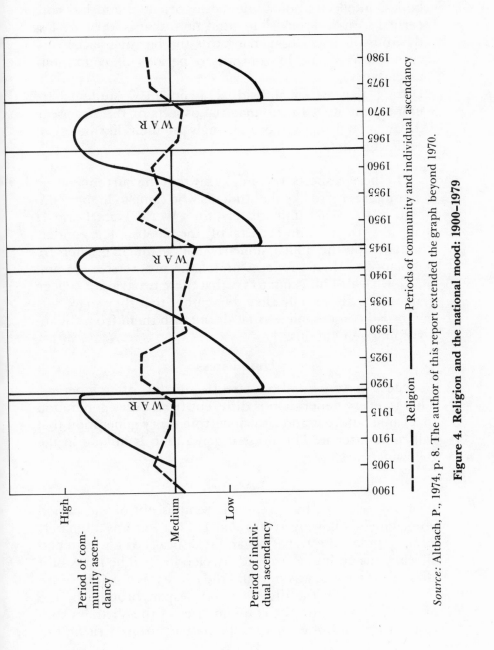

Source: Altbach, P., 1974, p. 8. The author of this report extended the graph beyond 1970.

Figure 4. Religion and the national mood: 1900–1979

- During periods of individual ascendancy, students tend to be less intellectual or academically oriented and less concerned with "relevance" in education; that is, they are less desirous of instruction that treats the burning social concerns of the day, in contrast to periods of community ascendancy.
- During periods of individual ascendancy, students are more committed to the material aspects of the American dream and believe more strongly in their likelihood of achieving them.

In these respects, one might say that the current college generation is more like the students who came to higher education in the years immediately after World Wars I and II than like their counterparts of the 1960s. The undergraduates of the 1960s similarly had a much greater resemblance to their predecessors of the progressive era and the New Deal. This is not to say that these two trios of college generations are exactly alike, but rather that they share certain broad commonalities that distinguish them from the intervening generations.

Uniqueness

College generations also share the quality of uniqueness. That is, every generation is different from every generation that came before it and probably from every generation that will come after it. The present generation is unique in the following ways:

The Times

In many respects, the present is reminiscent of the period immediately following World War I. That war was ultimately an unpopular one. What began idealistically as a war to end all wars turned into a costly, dirty bloodbath. The irony of it all is that the battle was won and the peace was lost. There are parallels between the divisions and despair brought by the First World War and the consequences of the Vietnam conflict. At the end of each war, the nation suffered rising unemployment and related economic woes. Soon after came White House scandals involving gross abuse of power within the executive branch. In the 1920s this abuse was known as Teapot Dome; in the 1970s its name was Watergate.

This is where the similarity ends. An economic upturn quickly followed World War I. The 1920s were hailed as the greatest period of prosperity in American history until they came to their crashing conclusion. In the 1970s economic conditions grew ever worse. By the time Teapot Dome saw the light of day, President Harding was dead, and little needed to be done. Watergate was not so easily dismissed. For more than a year, the country was forced to watch the scandal unfold, growing larger week by week, while the wheels of government ground slowly, ever so slowly, to the inevitable but not wholly satisfying conclusion.

The 1920s brought the nation a relatively restful interregnum. So did the 1950s. Both were periods of individual ascendancy. The seventies were different. The anticipated rest never came. What rest there was, was continually interrupted. In addition to Vietnam, Watergate, and persistent economic woes, there were an energy shortage, revelations of intelligence abuse at home and abroad, periodic hearings and convictions of government and industrial officials on charges of bribery and other criminal acts, crises in the Mideast, and a continuing perception that the nation's leaders were incapable of leading. That should probably read incapable of "managing," since the country seems more of a mind to rest than to follow.

When people are denied rest, they become irritable, anxious, apathetic, and disoriented. So do nations. Today, one sees these characteristics both in the country and in its college students. The post-1960s college generation has endured restlessness for a longer period than any other group in this century, with the possible exception of the depression/World War II cohort. This may help to explain the pervasive apathy among college students today as well as the Titanic mentality.

What this means for the future is uncertain. It is possi-

ble that the current mood will persist until the nation and its
students actually are able to rest or that the country and its
campuses will sleepily move on to the next cycle of activism
and reform. For instance, current student concern with nuclear energy and the draft may be either a well-publicized
ripple in a time of decreased student activism, like the
1977–78 South African divestment protests, or it could be
just the start of a new wave of activism, like the civil rights
and House Un-American Activities Committee demonstrations of the 1950s. It is impossible to know. There is no historical precedent in recent times for a restless period of
individual acendancy.

Size

The post-1960s college generation is the largest ever to enter
higher eduction. It is without a doubt more heterogenous in
background and experience than any of its predecessors.
There is to this extent less of a shared collegiate culture than
among previous generations. One obvious manifestation is
the decline in campus residential life. Diversity in academic
practice is another consequence. There is less college loyalty,
more transferring among schools, more variation in academic
ability, and a rise in nontraditional attendance patterns
beyond the pale of Monday-through-Friday nine-to-five
enrollment.

The large numbers of students have also created commonalities. The two most obvious are vocationalism and
competition. With more and more students in college and
recurring reports by government agencies that there are too
many college graduates for the number of jobs requiring college degrees, vocationalism and competition were virtually
guaranteed.

As for the future, college attendance rates have probably reached a saturation point among young people. Approximately one out of every two high school graduates will receive some form of higher education. The proportion of
older adults attending such institutions may increase, however. Colleges and universities are certainly working hard

enough to make this happen. In any case, higher education is no longer a growth industry. In prior times, enrollment grew in spite of demographic trends. Only war produced a drastic reduction in attendance. In the future, though, colleges will be slaves not only to demographics but also to changing economic conditions. As the number of older students grows, college enrollments will become more volatile. Enrollment among older students will increase when the employment market is poor and decrease when it improves. During the 1980s one can expect college enrollments to decrease, owing to the cresting of the post-World War II baby boom, and diversity will increase as minority attendance rates grow and as colleges make strenuous efforts to attract other nontraditional groups. Accordingly, the shared collegiate culture among students will probably decline even more, and attendance patterns will become increasingly diverse. Vocationalism and competition can be expected to decrease as the size of the college generation drops, but an economy that promises only limited growth should cause both to continue at a higher level than in previous times. Pressure on institutions to maintain or increase enrollment means that student basic skills will remain low, perhaps decrease even further, while cheating among undergraduates may rise as schools become increasingly loath to dismiss or crack down on students already enrolled.

Politics

Student political attitudes appeared to undergo a radical change from the 1920s to the 1930s, moving from right to left of the general public. In a 1924 nationwide straw poll, college students voted for Republican presidential candidate Calvin Coolidge in greater proportion than the country. In marked contrast, third-party progressive standard-bearer Robert LaFollette fared worse on campus than elsewhere. This is shown in Table 42. By the thirties, the picture had changed considerably. So says sociologist Seymour Martin Lipset (1976, pp. 178–179) who studied the student polls of the period. In a variety of surveys conducted at an assortment of

Table 42. Students, the public, and the election of 1924

Presidential candidates	National college straw poll	Actual election result
Calvin Coolidge, Republican	59%	54%
John W. Davis, Democrat	27	29
Robert M. LaFollette, Progressive	14	17

Source: *New Student,* November 1, 1924, p. 1. *Information Please Almanac,* 1979, p. 605.

campuses throughout the decade, "students expressed more liberal views toward economic planning and change than their counterparts before the depression. . . . Polls repeatedly showed that President Roosevelt was held in high regard among the younger generation." In fact, a 1935 *Literary Digest* survey found that college students across the country favored Roosevelt's policies by two to one.

This shift was not so much the result of a dramatic change in student attitudes as a dramatic change in the students themselves. Their numbers increased by 70 percent in a single decade, from 681,000 in 1922 to 1,154,000 in 1932. This expansion broadened public representation in higher education.

Throughout this century, students have tended to be more liberal politically than their parents. This was true even of the students who voted in the 1924 straw poll. It is just that their parents happened by and large to be very conservative Republicans, who were right of the rest of the nation. Consequently, even though the students were left of their parents, they still remained right of the country. With the near doubling of enrollments in the thirties, students represented a broader political spectrum. With that change, being left of students' parents also came to mean being left of the country.

The pattern continues today. In Chapter Three, it was noted that current undergraduates are more conservative politically and more liberal socially than the students of the 1960s. The fact of the matter is that, relative to the adult population, students today are almost exactly in the same place politically and socially that students were in the 1960s. This means that both students and the public shifted to more conservative political attitudes and more liberal social attitudes during the 1970s, but relative to one another there was little change. Students today remain just about as liberal politically and socially as they were a decade ago, in comparison to the general public. This is shown in Table 43.

Nonetheless, some very real differences distinguish the post-sixties generation from its predecessors. The current student cohort is more powerful politically both on and off campus than any student generation of the past. It is the first generation both to have the vote and to live in a time when the principle of in loco parentis is moribund. Politically, student organizations like PIRGs and lobbies are more powerful and effective than any of the groups that preceded them. The ultimate irony, though, is that, as the base of student political power expands with increasing enrollment, so does diversity, which brings to the current generation increasing division and less in common to work for politically, particularly on issues outside the educational realm. The meism that divides students politically will pass with time, but it seems quite likely that the diversity will increase for the next decade, with a concomitant decline in student political coherence and effectiveness.

Socialization

The family and the schools have had less influence in shaping today's college generation than its predecessors, unless, of course, one includes neglect as an influence. The media, particularly with the advent of home television and the growth of other nonprint forms, have played a greater role in shaping student attitudes than ever before, perhaps to a greater extent than was ever dreamed possible. The future promises a continuation of this trend.

Longevity

The post-1960s college generation will live longer than the students of preceding generations. This means that they will probably need and perhaps even want new types of

Table 43. Political and social attitudes of college students and adults

Issue	Freshmen	Undergraduates	Adults
Liberalize divorce laws	1969: 42% 1978: 49 +7		1968: 19% 1978: 24 +5
Oppose capital punishment		1969: 38% 1976: 36 −2	1969: 49 1978: 38 −11
Too much emphasis on rights of criminals	1969: 54 1978: 65 +11		1972: 74 1974: 88 +14
Legalize marijuana	1969: 26 1978: 50 +24		1969: 13 1978: 31 +18
Attend religious[a] services	1969: 89 1978: 86 −3		1969: 42 1978: 41 −1
Favor national service		1969: 52 1976: 36 −16	1969: 79 1977: 62 −17
Sympathies are with Israel in Mideast		1969: 79 1976: 70 −9	1969: 50 1976: 44 −6

[a]The question for students dealt with the last year, while the question for adults specified the preceding week.

Sources: ACE/UCLA Surveys, 1969, 1980. Carnegie Surveys 1969, 1976. Gallup Poll, 1969.

education—vocational instruction tied to longer careers, perhaps with more varied jobs comprising that career; knowledge and skills that will help them cope with a changing world; and postcollege instructional opportunities of all types, vocational as well as nonvocational.

A Recommendation

After all these facts and figures, what can one conclude about current college students? Most generally, that they form a special generation—like all others. More specifically, that on the average they are:

- self-concerned and me-oriented
- nonideological
- disenchanted with politics
- moderate in political attitudes
- liberal in social attitudes
- weak in basic skills
- career-oriented
- competitive
- diverse in lifestyles and background
- concerned with personal development (physical and spiritual)
- optimistic about their individual futures
- pessimistic about the future of the country
- interested in material success
- friendly and pleasant
- pragmatic

This generation is no better or no worse than any other. And despite its similarities to other generations, it is different.

From generational differences flow generational needs. The post-sixties college generation is in serious need of education with at least four distinctive qualities. It must be:

- Education that teaches the skills of reading, writing, arithmetic, speaking, problem solving, lifelong learning, "crap detecting" (identifying the drivel, exaggerations, and untruths that we hear and read each day), and surviving (coping with a rapidly changing environment). These skills are critical for a generation raised on the media, weak in the three Rs, and apt to live longer.

- Education which emphasizes our common humanity and which is concerned with our common problems and the ways that we together can solve them. This is ever so important in mitigating the self-concern that, more than any other characteristic, stands out in this generation.

- Education which stresses issues of value and questions of ethics. For a pragmatic, competitive generation with a Titanic mentality and a propensity for taking academic shortcuts, this is essential.

- And education which enlarges in two ways upon the vocational preparation this generation so desperately seeks. First, in serving much as the label on a bottle of medicine —telling when certain types of learning should be used, when they should not be used, and what the consequences of their misuse are likely to be. Second, in preparing students for a career, not a job. All too often, specialized technical training gives a student the knowledge to land a first job easily, but no means of mobility out of that job. One of the better-known engineering colleges in the country surveyed graduates a few years ago to find out what they thought of the education they had received. Alumni one or two years out of school complained that they had not been taught the newest technical skills and that they were forced to learn them on the job. Graduates five or more years out of school complained that they lacked the more general skills and abilities necessary to advance their careers and enrich their lives. Today's education should give students a base from which to continue learning and the skills necessary to perform well in a succession of jobs.

Such education can well be called liberal. But *liberal education,* like *general education,* is a buzzword that means different things to different people. Regardless of what we call it, this education needs to be distinguished from what it is not:

- First, whether labelled *liberal* or not, it is not esoteric, unworldly, or impractical. It is education for life which prepares people better for work, for leisure, for participation in the political process, and for coping with life's daily struggles. Any education which is not useful is useless. And there is nothing intrinsic to liberal education that requires it to be useless.

- Second, it is not a good without a market. Students and potential students may be dissatisfied with the general education programs they are currently required by their schools to take, but they do want a liberal education. Virtually all—97 percent of a representative sample of 1976 undergraduates—say that "a well-rounded general education" is an essential or fairly important element of a college education for them.

- Third, it is not out of step with the times. Too often, people think of liberal education as a luxury appropriate only for the leisure class, or perhaps for all students when economic times are good and jobs are plentiful. We all know that times are bad now. Yet the fact of the matter is that times have never been better for liberal education. Bad times obscure questions of ethics and values for us and thereby enhance the need for education to sensitize us to such questions; bad times heighten our sense of meism, attenuate our ties with the community, and thereby increase our need for education about human commonalities; bad times make competence in basic skills essential; and bad times make broad career training—more conducive for job change—a big plus. A common fear is that liberal education will dilute and cheapen career training or lengthen its course of study. This fear is unfounded.

- Fourth, this needed education is not merely a collection of assorted courses. Our society, and colleges in particular, tend to equate a liberal education with requirements that students take several courses each in a variety of subject fields—a little English, a little science, a little history, and so on. That is not liberal education. The totality of that kind of education amounts to little more than the sum of the individual courses, if to that. This approach lacks coherence and purpose, and few, if any, of the goals for liberal education outlined earlier are achieved thereby.

• Fifth, and finally, this education is not something that can be ignored until people themselves decide they want it. That just will not work. Several years after World War II, one of the scientists who worked on the atomic bomb project was asked whether he felt guilty about what he had accomplished. He said, "No! I feel as guilty as a tin can maker feels when a can is thrown through a window." Looming larger than the question of right or wrong was this person's isolation to such a large degree that he was unable to see or even think about the next step beyond his atomic theory work. Without liberal education, we as a society have the potential to educate a whole generation of like-minded people. Because the risks are substantial, liberal education simply cannot be ignored. Society is in the business of liberal education whether it means to be or not. By ignoring liberal education we teach our citizenry by example; through our every act and deed we teach the acceptable limits of misbehavior. Liberal education needs to be done well or it will be done poorly. It cannot be ignored.

At present we are doing poorly, very poorly indeed. Who is at fault? Who is to blame? The answer is simple— everyone. Everyone is at fault and everyone is to blame. Unfortunately, when everyone is responsible, no one is responsible. If everyone is to blame, then each of us can find someone else to fault. We have all failed at providing this essential education.

• Parents have failed. They are providing their children with more material comforts than ever before but with less of themselves. Both the quantity and quality of the time that parents spend with their children has been reduced. With this change, the parent is abdicating the role of teacher to others, often to unknown others. Part of the problem can be attributed to the growth of single-parent families, the lack of flexible work-time scheduling, and the unmet need for family support services. More disturbing and less remediable is what Daniel Yankelovich has called the growing "new breed" mentality—a laissez faire outlook based on parental self-concern and desire for self-fulfillment. New breed parents are more likely to believe "that children should be allowed to dress as they want, eat whatever is desired. . . , play with the kind of toys they want, and do pretty much whatever they want to." (Yankelovich, Skelly, and White, 1975, p. 32.) The lure of the new breed outlook for the 43 percent of parents who share it today is freedom and nonauthoritarian child raising, but the sad reality for the children of those families may be further neglect.

- The schools have failed. The education advocated here is too precious to be reserved solely for the college-educated; yet it is clear that the schools of the nation are not providing it. In fact, college admission test scores, the National Assessment of Educational Progress, and a College Board blue-ribbon inquiry indicate that schools today are doing a worse job than schools did in the past. Students are graduating unschooled in the three Rs and other survival skills. They are graduating without skills in dealing with issues of values and questions of ethics. They are graduating unschooled in our common heritage and problems. And they are graduating unschooled in career education.

- Television has failed. Television is the greatest educational experiment ever attempted. Increasingly, it performs roles once filled by the family, the schools, and the church. But television does not provide liberal education. In fact, it lies. During the past three decades, television has provided America with a distorted image of itself, alternating the idealized and the sordid. It has minimized the contribution of women, minorities, the aged, and the handicapped to our society. It has exalted violence and enshrined commercial values. For all problems there is a product, and for every product there is a problem that is solved. Instead of educating the young, television has sold them products, junk food as well as drugs, and socialized them for a consumer society. It has fostered in the young a jaundiced and more fearful view of the society than is warranted. It has pandered to the public mood. In this post-Watergate/ Proposition 13 era—a time when social trust is low and when people are quick to suspect wrongdoing, a time when the public desperately needs to know the good that is being done—television has responded with the investigative reporting, the muckraking, and the exposes that were so badly needed in the 1950s and 1960s but which never materialized then. Television is not evil. It is simply a commercial enterprise. Television is not an educational tool, either. If we want it to be different, we need to make government aware that we do. The Federal Communications Commission and other forums already provide us with opportunities to talk back to our television sets, but the public has not chosen to use these channels.

- Youth celebrities have failed. During a football game this past season, a television commercial featured a well-known and popular athlete arguing persuasively for the public to support a charitable cause. As it happened, he was playing in the game that resumed after the ad. A short time after play began, the star of the commercial engaged in unusually rough and unsportsmanlike conduct. His team was penalized and his behavior was shown twice in slow motion on television. The fellow was next heard from during contract negotiation season. As the local sportscaster told the story, it seems that the athlete wanted a raise over what already sounded like a great deal of money and he threatened to retire unless he got it. What does one learn from this fellow—the importance of helping others, as advocated in the commercial, or the importance of looking out for number one? Not all celebrities resemble this one, but a number do. Perhaps that is why the youth heroes of the 1960s have become the celebrities of the 1970s and why the bookstore biography sections of the 1960s have become the people sections of the 1970s.

- Government has failed. Government is an educator,

though not of late a liberal educator. The lessons of Vietnam and Watergate discussed in Chapter Three were not only crushing but inimical to the concept of a liberal education. Little has been done to revise these lessons or reteach them in the years since; instead, they have been reinforced —taught again and again.

The most serious consequence of the Vietnam/ Watergate era is not the cynicism, the decreasing interest in politics, or even the turning inward of young people but rather the death of altruism. Service became a dirty word, associated as it was with a dirty war and a self-serving administration. One need only recall the response of White House staffer Gordon Strachen when he was asked what advice he would give to young people interested in government. He told them, "Stay out." At a time when people feel they are being victimized, when individual concern for others is low, and when understanding of our shared heritage, problems, and solutions is waning, public service is a critical need. This nation must move toward universal service for young people 16 to 24 years of age as a partial remedy to these problems. Service is also a step away from the sense of entitlement that is so widespread today. Service places the emphasis on responsibility to others and on active participation in society. Opportunities to spend a year or more helping others and providing community service should be created at the local level through the action of both the public and the private sector. Regional boards should develop, coordinate, evaluate, counsel, and disseminate information about such activities. At the national level, a public service corporation should be created. It would be the job of that corporation to establish national policy, coordinate local activities, develop multiregional and international programs, and maintain centralized records. Incentives for young people to participate must be strong. Motivators should include educational credit, tuition support, preference for college admission and jobs, useful experience, and in-service education. The actual salary paid to volunteers should be set at the subsistence level. It would be desirable if, within a few years, public service had become not only something that young people looked forward to but also a social norm, a responsibility of citizenship in our society.

This would be liberal education at its best, but liberal education is out of favor with government today. It tends to be thought of as a luxury inappropriate in an era of financial conservatism. In its stead, the emphasis is placed on practical education. In truth, though, what could be more practical for the individual or the society than a liberal education or a liberally educated populace?

• Finally, colleges have failed. Colleges talk a good deal about liberal education and are considered the prime locale for its teaching, but few colleges provide it. Today there is an increasing tendency among institutions to cater to the educational marketplace rather than to offer or require what the public needs. Vocational training is in vogue. Most colleges have relegated liberal education to a shrinking portion of their curriculum called general education, which the Carnegie Foundation (1977, p. 11) has described as "a disaster area . . . on the defensive and losing ground for more than 100 years." General education programs tend to be staffed by faculty who are ill prepared to teach in them and who in any case have little interest in doing so. Rewards for faculty participation vary from small to negative. General education programs are more often a reflection of an institution's economic and political needs than of its educational mission. The courses that are offered under the rubric of general education have little to do with the goals of liberal education as discussed earlier. More often they seek to impart the body of knowledge associated with a particular subject matter—French, art, or mathematics.

Some schools do a better job than others in providing a liberal education. St. John's College in Annapolis, Maryland, and Santa Fe, New Mexico, for instance, offers an excellent program based on the great books. However, the classical approach to liberal education is not the only one that works. Scripps College in Claremont, California offers an exemplary contemporary program called a humanities internship, which touches upon all of the goals discussed for liberal education. Many institutions of higher education are floundering as a consequence of today's adverse demographic and economic conditions. Liberal education can be a realistic way for them to save themselves.

It is important to remember, though, that a few courses do not make for a liberal education. Liberal education must be an element in every course that a school offers. Each course should be concerned with basic skills and touch upon the place of its subject matter in the larger world. Liberal education must be an element in every interaction between students and teachers and in every new administrative policy that a school formulates. To permit academic dishonesty by students to go unchecked or for institutions themselves to engage in unfair practices in academic, financial aid, admissions, or advertising concerns which are, according to the Carnegie Council (Carnegie Council on Policy Studies in Higher Education, 1979), on the rise, teaches students as much about the world as any course a college can offer, if not more.

We—all of us—have to do better at liberal education. Many creative approaches to improved education are possible, and any number of them can show that the education needed for today can be vibrant, attract students, and get students jobs. As one example, consider an approach focused on social problem solving: a rigorous four-year undergraduate program with the following characteristics:

• The entire first year would be spent studying a common interdisciplinary core on the theme of social issues or problems. The core would rely upon a combination of lectures, seminars, and tutorials, rather than a collection of traditional courses. Particular attention would be given to instruction in writing, speaking, research, and problem-solving skills.

- Students would major in a problem area, such as health, the cities, hunger and nutrition, criminal justice, or the environment, and minor in a discipline like economics, sociology, biology, art, or English.
- Students would spend one full semester and two summers in career-related internships. They would enroll in a preparation seminar before entering the internship and in a return seminar after completing it. A placement office would be an integral part of the program.
- Students would be required to write a senior thesis in a social problem area, defend the thesis, and pass a senior-year comprehensive examination in order to graduate.

Basic skills—writing, speaking, research, and problem solving—would be stressed. During the first year, a paper and an oral presentation would be required each week.

General education would be the focus of the first-year program. The common interdisciplinary core would represent a coherent and integrated approach to general education, buttressed by the senior comprehensive examination, which would require students to review, reassess, and make new connections in what they have studied during their college years.

The program would offer broad career preparation in areas such as health and criminal justice. Basic skills instruction would stress a variety of tools or skills necessary and directly transferable to many occupations. Students would spend the equivalent of one academic year in career-related internships, providing them the opportunity to apply classroom learning to the world of work. It would also allow them to test possible vocations before making a career choice.

Social problems and ethical concerns would be the heart of the program. Even if graduates chose not to work in the public sector, and many would not, they would nonetheless receive an education that immersed them in questions of ethics and values and that equipped them for informed participation in our society.

The program would have three obvious advantages for

any institution adopting it. First, it would respond to student and parent vocational concerns in the context of the liberal arts, where enrollments are now declining. Second, it should reduce the cost of undergraduate instruction, by replacing the larger number of courses currently being offered with a common freshman core. And third, the potential excellence of the college's graduates, the rigor of the college program, and the skills which it seeks to teach should make its students quite desirable from an employer's point of view, and make the college quite desirable from a student's point of view.

Such an approach is but one path to reforming liberal education. Other paths are equally easy to see. We merely need to follow them. The future of our world and the next college generation depends on it.

Appendix A

Studies Used in this Report

The Carnegie Commission and the Carnegie Council have undertaken several studies related to this book. They are referred to in this volume as Carnegie Surveys, 1969; Carnegie Surveys, 1976; Carnegie Surveys, 1978, and Carnegie Study, 1979.

The Carnegie Surveys, 1969 were conducted under the auspices of the Carnegie Commission on Higher Education with the cooperation of the American Council on Education and support from the U.S. Office of Education. They probed the opinions and experiences of 60,000 faculty, 70,000 undergraduates, and 30,000 graduate students. The technical details of the survey and the survey questionnaires can be found in *Teachers and Students: Aspects of American Higher Education,* edited by Martin Trow (New York: McGraw-Hill, 1975).

The Carnegie Surveys, 1976 were conducted by the Carnegie Council on Policy Studies in Higher Education and involved 25,000 faculty members, 25,000 undergraduates, and 25,000 graduate students. The questions used in these surveys and the survey details are discussed in a *Technical Report: 1975 Carnegie Council National Surveys of Higher Education,* by Judy Roizen, Oliver Fulton, and Martin Trow (Berkeley, Calif.: Center for Studies in Higher Education, University of California, 1978).

The Carnegie Surveys, 1978 were conducted under the auspices of the Carnegie Council and involved a comprehensive study of how a representative sample of 586 two- and four-year colleges and universities were adapting to the 1970s. Three questionnaires were sent to participating institutions—one for the president, one for an institutional research officer or similar administrator, and one for a student affairs staff member. The details of the survey are reported in a technical report by Sura Johnson, *Survey of Institutional Adaptations* (Berkeley, Calif.: Carnegie Council on Policy Studies in Higher Education, 1979).

The Carnegie Study, 1979 involved visits to campuses of twenty-six institutions that participated in the 1978 survey: College of New Rochelle, College of Staten Island, Columbia University, Eckerd College, Emory University, Evergreen State College, Florida Atlantic University, Georgia Institute of Technology, Georgia State University, Hunter College, Kansas Wesleyan College, Kean College of New Jersey, New York University, Northwest Missouri State University, Oklahoma Baptist University, St. Gregory's College, State University of New York at Old Westbury, Trinity College, University of Houston, University of La Verne, University of Miami, University of Missouri-Columbia, University of Oregon, University of Tulsa, Webster College, and Whittier College. These institutions characterize the diversity of the original sample. At each school, the individuals who completed the questionnaires in the 1978 survey or designated substitutes were interviewed, with the exception of the student personnel administrators. In place of the latter, a student leader, a student government official or a campus newspaper editor, and a group of between six and ten intentionally diverse undergraduates were queried, using a standard list of questions. In all, 182 students participated in the group interviews. Bulletin boards and student posters were examined, and student newspapers were collected at each school as well.

Another major source of data used in this volume was collected under the auspices of the Cooperative Institutional Research Program of the American Council on Education and the University of California at Los Angeles. Since 1966, a representative sample of first-time full-time college fresh-

men has been surveyed annually. The number of participating colleges has ranged from about 400 to more than
1,000. Reports of the results are published each year. These
reports and information about them are available from the
Cooperative Institutional Research Program, Laboratory for
Research in Higher Education, Graduate School of Education, University of California, Los Angeles, California 90024.

Appendix B

Carnegie Typology of Colleges and Universities

In Chapter Three, the Carnegie typology of institutions of higher education is used in Table 15. The typology is indirectly used in other parts of this book, as will be explained. This typology distinguishes nine institutional types. They are described as follows in the Carnegie Council report *A Classification of Institutions of Higher Education: Revised Edition* (Berkeley, Calif., 1978).

Doctorate-Granting Institutions

- *Research Universities I.* These institutions numbered among the 50 leading universities in federal financial support of academic science in at least two of the three academic years 1972–73, 1973–74, and 1974–75, provided they awarded at least 50 Ph.D.s (plus M.D.s if a medical school was on the same campus) in 1973–74. Rockefeller University was included because of the high quality of its research and doctoral training, although it did not meet these criteria. These 50 universities are also referred to in this book as "the most research-oriented universities" and as "the most prestigious research universities."

- *Research Universities II.* These universities numbered among the 100 leading institutions in federal financial support in at least two of the three years identified above and awarded at least 50 Ph.D.s (plus M.D.s if a medical school was on the same campus) in 1973–74. At least 25 of the 50 degrees had to have been Ph.D.s. Under an alternate criterion, the institution was one of the 60 institutions leading in the total number of Ph.D.s awarded during the years between 1965–66 and 1974–75. In addition, a few institutions which did not quite meet these criteria but which did have graduate programs of high quality and showed impressive promise for future development are included here.

• *Doctorate-Granting Universities I.* These institutions awarded 40 or more Ph.D.s in at least five fields in 1973–74 (plus M.D.s if a medical school was on the same campus) or received at least $3 million in total federal support in either 1973–74 or 1974–1975. No institution is included that granted less than 20 Ph.D.s in at least five fields (plus M.D.s if a medical school was on the same campus) regardless of the amount of federal financial support that it received.

• *Doctorate-Granting Universities II.* These institutions awarded at least 20 Ph.D.s in 1973–74 without regard to field or 10 Ph.D.s in at least three fields. In addition, a few institutions have been included that may be expected to increase the number of Ph.D.s awarded within a few years.[1]

Comprehensive Universities and Colleges

• *Comprehensive Universities and Colleges I.* These institutions offered both a liberal arts program and several other programs, such as engineering and business administration. Many of them awarded master's degrees, but they either lacked a doctoral program or had an extremely limited doctoral program. All institutions in this group had at least two professional or occupational programs and enrolled at least 2,000 students in 1976. If an institution's enrollment was smaller than this, it was not considered very comprehensive.

• *Comprehensive Universities and Colleges II.* This group includes state colleges and private colleges that offered a lib-

---

[1]In all cases, the term Ph.D. should be understood as including the Ed.D. and other doctor's degrees.

eral arts program and at least one professional or occupational program, such as teacher training or nursing. Many
of the institutions in this group are former teachers' colleges
that have broadened their programs to include a liberal arts
curriculum. In general, private institutions with fewer than
1,500 students and public institutions with fewer than 1,000
students in 1976 were not included, even if they offered a
selection of programs, because they could not be regarded
as comprehensive with such small enrollments. Instead,
such institutions were classified as liberal arts colleges.

Liberal Arts Colleges

- *Liberal Arts Colleges I.* These colleges scored 1,030 or more
on a selectivity index developed by Alexander W. Astin[2] or
were included among the 200 baccalaureate-granting institutions leading in numbers of graduates receiving Ph.D.s
at 40 leading doctorate-granting institutions between 1920
and 1966 (National Academy of Sciences, *Doctorate Recipi-
ents from United States Universities, 1958–1966,* Washington,
D.C., 1967, Appendix B). These institutions are sometimes
referred to in this volume as "the most selective liberal arts
colleges."
- *Liberal Arts Colleges II.* These institutions include all the liberal arts colleges that did not meet the criteria for inclusion
in the first group of liberal arts colleges. Again, the distinc-
tion between liberal arts and comprehensive is not clear-cut
for some of the larger colleges in this group, so in part it
was a matter of judgment.

Two-Year Colleges and Institutes

- *Community and Junior Colleges.*

[2]It is based on average verbal and mathematical SAT scores of entering freshmen as
reported in several institutional directories of the early 1970s. The index has not
been published, but it is available on tape from the Higher Education Research
Institute, Los Angeles.

References

ABC News-Harris Survey. "Confidence in Most Institutions Down." Vol. I, Ch.27. March 5, 1979.

ACE/UCLA Survey, 1969. (See Creager and others, 1969.)

ACE/UCLA Survey, 1979. (See Astin and others, 1980.)

Adelson, J., and O'Neil, R. "Growth of Political Ideas in Adolescence: The Sense of Community." In A. Orum (Ed.), *The Seeds of Politics: Youth and Politics in America*. Englewood Cliffs, N. J.: Prentice-Hall, 1972.

Advisory Panel on the Scholastic Aptitude Test Score Decline. *On Further Examination*. New York: College Entrance Examination Board, 1977.

Altbach, P. *Student Politics in America: A Historical Analysis*. New York: McGraw-Hill, 1974

American Council on Education. *A Fact Book on Higher Education*. Washington, D.C.: American Council on Higher Education, 1977.

Arterton, F. C. "The Impact of Watergate on Children's Attitudes Toward Political Authority." In D. Caraley (Ed.), *American Political Institutions in the 1970's*. New York: Columbia University Press, 1976.

Astin, A. W. and others. *The American Freshman: National Norms for Fall 1979*. Los Angeles: Cooperative Institutional Research Program, Laboratory for Research in Higher Education. Graduate School of Education, University of California, 1980.

Bachman, J., and Johnston, L. D. "The Freshman, 1979."*Psychology Today*, 1979, *13* (4), 79–87.

Bachman, J., Johnston, L. D., and O'Malley, P. *Monitoring the Future: Questionnaire Response from the Nation's High School Seniors, 1976*. Ann Arbor: Institute for Social Research, University of Michigan, 1980a.

Bachman, J., Johnston, L. D., and O'Malley, P. *Monitoring the Future: Questionnaire Response from the Nation's High School Seniors, 1978*. Ann Arbor: Institute for Social Research, University of Michigan, 1980b.

Bane, M. J. "Marital Disruption and Lives of Children." *Journal of Social Issues*, 1976, *32* (1), 109–110.

Baritz, L. (Ed.). *The Culture of the Twenties*. Indianapolis, Ind.: Bobbs-Merrill, 1970.

Better Homes and Gardens (Eds.). *A Report on the American Family*. Des Moines, Iowa: Meredith, 1972.

Blackburn, R. T., and others. *Changing Practices in Undergraduate Education*.

Berkeley, Calif.: Carnegie Council on Policy Studies in Higher Education, 1976.

Bow, J. "Davis, the Only U. C. Campus with Honor System, Prepares to Revise Its Code," *Sacramento Bee,* August 3, 1975, p. D-5.

Bronfenbrenner, U. *Two Worlds of Childhood: U.S.-U.S.S.R..* New York: Russell Sage Foundation, 1970.

Brooks, T., and Marsh, E. *The Complete Directory to Prime Time Network TV Shows.* New York: Ballantine Books, 1979.

Browne, H. *How You Can Profit From a Monetary Crisis.* New York: Macmillan, 1974.

Brubacher, J. S., and Willis, R. *Higher Education in Transition: A History of American Colleges and Universities 1636–1976.* (3rd ed.) New York: Harper & Row, 1976.

Bureau of the Census. U.S. Department of Commerce. *Historical Statistics of the U.S.: Statistical Abstracts.* Washington, D.C.: U.S. Government Printing Office, 1975.

Cain, L. D. "The 1916–1925 Cohort of Americans: Its Contributions to the Generation Gap." Paper presented at annual meeting of the American Sociological Association, Washington, D.C., September 1, 1970.

Carnegie Council on Policy Studies in Higher Education. *Fair Practices in Higher Education: Rights and Responsibilities of Students and Their Colleges in a Period of Intensified Competition for Enrollments.* San Francisco: Jossey-Bass, 1979.

Carnegie Foundation for the Advancement of Teaching.*Twenty-ninth Annual Report,* New York: Carnegie Foundation for the Advancement of Teaching, 1935.

Carnegie Foundation for the Advancement of Teaching. *Missions of the College Curriculum: A Contemporary Review with Suggestions.* San Francisco: Jossey-Bass, 1977.

Carnegie Studies, 1979. See Appendix A.

Carnegie Surveys, 1969, 1976, 1978. See Appendix A.

Chandler, R. *Public Opinion: A CBS News Reference Book.* New York: Bowker, 1972.

"College Students Found Dependent on Cars." *Chronicle of Higher Education,* 1979, *19,* 2.

Creager, J. A., and others. *National Norms for Entering College Freshmen –Fall 1969.* Washington, D.C.: American Council on Education, 1969.

DeCecco, J. P., and Richards, A. K. "Study of Student Perceptions of Civic Education," *Journal of Social Issues,* 1975, *31* (2), 111–121.

Doyle, L., and Freding, M. "Comic." *Nutshell,* 1979/80, p. 172.

Dyer, W. *Your Erroneous Zones.* New York: Funk & Wagnalls, 1976.

Dyer, W. *Pulling Your Own Strings.* New York: Funk & Wagnalls, 1978.

"Eight in 10 College Students Use Alcohol, Study Finds." *Chronicle of Higher Education,* October 29, 1979, p.2.

Elder, G. H. *Children of the Great Depression.* Chicago: University of Chicago Press, 1974.

Erdman, P. E. *The Crash of '79.* New York: Simon & Schuster, 1976.

Erikson, E. H. *Childhood in Society.* New York: Norton, 1963.

Fitzgerald, F. S. *This Side of Paradise.* New York: Scribner's, 1920.

Friday, N. *My Mother/My Self.* New York: Delacorte, 1977.

Fuller, B., and Samuelson, J. "Student Votes: Do They Make a Difference?" Washington, D.C.: U.S. Student Association,1977.

Gallup International, Inc. *Gallup Opinion Index: Report 1969.* Princeton, N.J.: Gallup International, Inc., 1969.

Gerbner, G., and Gross, L. "Group Finds Less Violence on TV." *San Francisco Chronicle,* August 16, 1979, p. 47.

Getting Your Share: Social Security, Medicare, Government Benefits. New York: Simon & Schuster, 1977.

Goulden, J. *The Best Years 1945–1950.* New York: Atheneum, 1976.

"Growing Skepticism About Public Leaders . . . and Rising Doubts About Government Waste." *Public Opinion,* March–April, 1978, p. 23.

Haley, A. *Roots.* New York: Doubleday, 1976.

Harris, L., and Associates. "Confidence in Institutions." *The Harris Survey,* January 5, 1978.

Harris, L.,and Associates, "High Confidence in Institutions." *The Harris Survey,* March 5, 1979.

Hendrick, C., and Murfin, M. I. "Project Library Ripoff: Study of Periodical Mutilation in University Library," *College and Research Libraries,* 1974, *35,* 402–411.

Hershey, M. R., and Hill, D. B. "Watergate and Presidents: Attitudes Toward the President," *American Journal of Political Science,* 1975, *19* (4), 703–726.

Hoffman, F. J. *The 20s: American Writing in the Postwar Decade.* New York: Free Press, 1965.

Hofstadter, R. *The Age of Reform.* New York: Vintage Books, 1960.

Hollander, N. "Adolescents and the War: The Sources of Socialization." *Journalism Quarterly,* 1971, *48,* 472–479.

Information Please Almanac, 1979. Los Angeles: S & S Enterprises, 1979.

Jacobson, D. *Student Voting Power.* Washington, D.C. United States Student Association, 1978.

"Johns Hopkins Scraps Honor Code." *Los Angeles Times,* July 28, 1975, p.2.

Johnston, L. D., and Bachman, J. *Monitoring the Future: Questionnaire Responses from the Nation's High School Seniors, 1975.* Ann Arbor: Institute for Social Research, University of Mighican, 1980.

Johnston, L. D., Bachman, J., and O'Malley, P. *Monitoring the Future: Questionnaire Responses from the Nation's Higher Scool Seniors,* 1977. Ann Arbor: Institute for Social Research, University of Michigan, 1980.

Kanter, R. M. *Commitment and Community: Communes and Utopias in Sociological Perspective.* Cambridge, Mass.:Harvard University Press, 1972.

Keniston, K., and The Carnegie Council on Children. *All Our Children: The American Family Under Pressure.* New York: Harcourt Brace Jovanovich, 1977.

Kohlbeig, L. "Moral Development and Identification." In H. W. Stevenson (Ed.), *Child Phychology 62nd Yearbook, National Society for the Study of Education.* Part 1. Chicago: University of Chicago Press, 1963.

Lamont, L. *Campus Shock.* New York: Dutton, 1979.

Lasch, C. "The Narcissist Society." *New York Review of Books,* 1976, *23* (15), 5–13.

Lasch, C. *The Culture of Narcissism.* New York: Norton, 1979.

Lee, C. B. T. *The Campus Scene, 1900–1970: Changing Styles in Undergraduate Life*. New York: McKay, 1970.

Leuchtenburg, W. *The Perils of Prosperity: 1914–1932*. Chicago: University of Chicago Press, 1958.

Levine, A. *Handbook on Undergraduate Curriculum*. San Francisco: Jossey-Bass, 1978.

Lipset, S. M. *Rebellion in the University*. Chicago: University of Chicago Press, 1976.

Lipsius, M. "Campuses Help Pave the Road to Gold." *Programming*, December-January, 1979.

"Louis Harris Finds Rising Alienation." *Public Opinion*, May–June, 1978, p. 23.

Lyle, J. and Hoffman, H. R. "Television Viewing by Pre-school-age Children." In R. Brown (Ed.), *Children and Television*. Beverly Hills, Calif.: Sage, 1976.

Marin, P. "The New Narcissism." *Harpers Magazine*, 1975, *251* (1505), 45–46.

Michaelis, D. "The New Youth." *Life*, 1977, Special Issue, p. 26.

Monsky, M. *Looking Out for Number One*. New York: Simon & Schuster, 1975.

Morgentau, T. and Doyle, J. "Mood of a Nation: P. Cadell's Poll." *Newsweek*, August 6, 1979, pp. 26–27.

Mowry, G. I. *The Era of Theodore Roosevelt and the Birth of Modern America 1900–1912*. New York: Harper & Row, 1962.

National Assessment of Educational Progress. *Change in Political Knowledge and Attitudes, 1969–76*. Washington, D.C.: National Center for Education Statistics, 1978.

National Center for Education Statistics, *Opening Fall Enrollment, 1969*. Washington, D.C.: U.S. Government Printing Office, 1969.

National Center for Education Statistics. *Opening Fall Enrollment, 1979*. Washington, D.C.: U.S. Government Printing Office, 1979.

"National Crime Wave Plagues University Libraries," *Chronicle of Higher Education*, August 2, 1976, p. 5.

National On-Campus Report, May 1978.

National On-Campus Report, October 1978.

National On-Campus Report, February 1979.

National On-Campus Report, March 1979.

National On-Campus Report, June 1979.

National On-Campus Report, July 1979.

National On-Campus Report, October 1979.

New Student, Nov. 1, 1924.

Nordheimer, J.. "The Family in Transition: A Challenge from Within." *New York Times*, November 27, 1977, p. 7.

Peterson, I. "Race for Grades Revives Among College Students: Cheating and Anxiety Rise." *New York Times*, November 21, 1974, p. 1.

Peterson R., and Bilorusky J. A. *May 1970: The Campus Aftermath of Cambodia and Kent State*. Berkeley, Calif.: Carnegie Council on Policy Studies in Higher Education, 1971.

Piaget, J. *The Moral Judgement of the Child*. New York: Collier, 1962. (Originally published 1932.)

Pomper, G. *The Election of 1976*. New York: McKay, 1977.

Public Opinion, May-June 1978, p. 2.

Public Opinion, March-April 1978, p. 23.

Public Opinion, March-May 1979, p. 22.

Public Opinion, April-May 1980, p. 21.

Ringer, R. J. *Winning Through Intimidation.* New York: Fawcett World, 1976.

Rodgers, J. R., Jr., and Lewis, E. B. "Student Attitudes Toward Mr. Nixon: The Consequences of Negative Attitudes Toward a President for Political System Support." *American Politics Quarterly,* 1975, *3* (4), 423-436.

Rudolph, F. *The American College and University: A History.* New York: Vintage Books, 1962.

Sheehy, G. *Passages.* New York: Dutton, 1976.

Smith, M. J. *When I Say No, I Feel Guilty.* New York: Bantam Books, 1975.

"Student Groups Fund Law Suits." *National On-Campus Report,* July 1979, p. 1.

"The College Student." *Fortune,* 1936, *13* (6).

The Spectrum, State University of New York at Buffalo, New York.

"The Wild Young People by One of Them." *The Atlantic Monthly,* September 1920.

"13,000 Turkeys Commit Suicide." *San Francisco Chronicle,* December 14, 1979, p. 3.

Tiger, L. *Optimism: The Biology of Hope.* New York: Simon & Schuster, 1979.

Todd, L. "What's Hot and What's Not." *Programming,* December-January 1978.

"Vandals Are Keeping Busy." *New York Times,* March 27, 1977, p. 7.

Wecter, D. *The Age of the Great Depression 1929–1941: A History of American Life.* New York: Viewpoints, 1975.

White, T. *Breach of Faith: The Fall of Richard Nixon.* New York: Atheneum, 1975.

Winn, M. *The Plug-in Drug.* New York: Bantam Books, 1977.

Wohl, R. *The Generation of 1914.* Cambridge, Mass.: Harvard University Press, 1970.

Wolfe, T. *Mauve Gloves and Madmen, Clutter and Vine.* New York: Bantam Books, 1977.

Wuthnow, R. "The New Religions in Social Context." In C. Globe and R. Bellah (Eds.), *The New Religious Consciousness.* Berkeley: University of California Press, 1976.

Yankelovich, D. *The Changing Values on Campus: Political and Personal Attitudes of Today's College Students.* New York: Washington Square Press, 1972.

Yankelovich, D. *The New Morality: A Profile of American Youth in the 70s.* New York: McGraw-Hill, 1974.

Yankelovich, Skelly, and White, Inc. *The General Mills American Family Report, 1974–1975: A Study of the American Family and Money.* Minneapolis, Minn.: General Mills, 1975.

Youth in Turmoil. New York: A Fortune Book, Time-Life Books, 1969.

Index